Praise for
The Totally Awesome Money Book for Kids (and their Parents)

Nominated by the American Library Association as a "Best Book for Young Adults for 1994".

"A perfect book for kids who want to know what they can do with their money…plenty of examples throughout. I liked being shown easy ways to keep your own budget. One really good section was advice on short and long term goals."
—*New York Newsday*

"The principle here is that if the basics of money are learned young they become commonplace and nonthreatening….The tone is thoroughly kid-like….Overall, smart, cheerful, and sensible."
—*Kirkus Reviews*

"A fun and fact-filled guide about the basics of saving, investing, borrowing, working and taxes."
—*ABC Classroom Connection*

"A comprehensive look at finances in a style that is just right for kids. The chapters are short and to the point. The information is easy to access and easy to understand…a good solid foundation for kids."
—*VOYA (Voice of Youth Advocates)*

The Totally Awesome
BUSINESS
BOOK
for Kids

The Totally Awesome
BUSINESS
BOOK
for Kids

with Twenty Super Businesses
You Can Start Right Now!

**Adriane G. Berg
and
Arthur Berg Bochner**

Newmarket Press
New York

To all the kids
in this world who've had bad breaks.
Hang in there—you'll make your own luck.

95 96 97 10 9 8 7 6 5 4 3 2 1

Library of Congress Cataloging-in-Publication Data
Berg, Adriane G.
The totally awesome business book for kids:with 20 super businesses you can start right now! / by Adriane G. Berg and Arthur Berg Bochner
        p.   cm.
Includes bibliographical references and index.
ISBN 1-55704-229-2 (hc)   ISBN 1-55704-226-8 (pb)
1. Small business—Management—Juvenile literature. 2. New business enter-prises—Management—Juvenile literature 3. Money-making projects for children [1. Moneymaking projects. 2. Business enterprises. 3. Entrepreneurship.] I. Bochner, Arthur Berg. II. Title.
HD62.7.B64   1995
658 .041—dc20   95-7688
                                             CIP
                                             AC
Quantity Purchases
Companies, professional groups, clubs, and other organizations may qualify for special terms when ordering quantities of this title. For information contact: Special Sales Department, Newmarket Press, 18 East 48th Street, New York, NY 10017, or call (212) 832-3575.

Book Design by Deborah Daly
First Edition
MANUFACTURED IN THE UNITED STATES OF AMERICA

Contents

PART 1
Business:
The Big Picture

PART 2
Business Skills:
Everyday Things You Have to Know to Run Your Business

Letter to Kids

Dear Kids,

When I was eleven my mom and I wrote a book called *The Totally Awesome Money Book for Kids and Their Parents.* It explained how the stock market works, what banks can do for you, how to make a budget, and even how to invest money in other countries.

I traveled all over the United States, to England, and to lots of schools to talk about investing. It was great. Kids learned how to read the stock pages, buy mutual funds, and save for college. Best of all, they liked learning of methods to buy one share of stock in companies they know, like McDonalds, Toys "R" Us, and Burger King.

But, many of my personal friends and kids I met at the schools asked me "How do I make the money to do all the cool stuff you wrote about in your book?" I thought about that, too.

The best way I know to have money without someone giving it to you is by getting a job or running a business. I am too young to get a job (no one will hire me, and if they would, it's illegal because of child labor laws). So, I decided to start a business and write about the things I learned.

If you are curious, my business is selling Magic the Gathering cards through retailers. I buy packs of these collectible cards, sort them, price them, and place them in retail stores in my neighborhood. I earn about $30 to $80 a week, which boils down to $20 to $60 after expenses.

You see there is a lot to being in business, even a small one like mine. You have to think of a way to make money that works, find people to work with, get supplies, be on time, keep records, speak up for yourself, use the telephone, and do many other big and little tasks.

I guess that's what being a business owner (it's also called being an *entrepreneur*) is all about. Adults find that being an entrepreneur is hard to do, but it can actually be very easy for kids like us and lots of fun, too. In this book, you will learn some vital skills that are important to running a successful business. Of all the things that will be important to you in later life, the most important skill you'll learn is how to get the *big picture*. More about that later.

After that, you will learn about businesses that you can start right now, including many that can help to save the environment. I am very concerned about the environment, and I think that you are, too. That's one of the reasons I wrote this book.

At least ten of the businesses described help stop waste or are environmentally sound in other ways. None pollute the environment. For example, one of the businesses in this book is bringing some of your recyclable goods to the recycling plant for a profit. Also, there is a business in which you learn to grow your own plants for a profit. This helps you to make money while saving the environment.

Both my publisher and my mom are very interested in getting across ideas about how businesses are formed and how they make money. I agree. But of more importance to me is starting out with a worthy idea—an idea that not only works and makes money, but also does some good in the world. If nobody is benefiting from what you do and many are harmed, I don't call that business a success, no matter how much money it makes.

I think this is more important to kids than adults think. I'd like to hear from you about that. What businesses have you started? Did they make money? Did they help others? What is your most important goal in going into business? You can tell me by writing to my company:

Sneakers and Suits
143 WS Route 206 S.
Chester, NJ 17930

If you are worried about getting bored while reading this book, don't be. This book is filled with activities and cartoon characters to keep you interested and entertained as you read. Also, this book is written by me, a kid, so it will be simple to understand.

Before we even start, I can think of three questions you might want to ask already:

1. What's that big picture that you have been talking about, Arthur?

The *big picture* is seeing all the important things about a business at once. When I look at a business project, I look at everything. I look at the cost of the business and where I can get the supplies that I need to run it successfully. I also look at the way that the business would work in my area. I see if the business needs anybody else besides me to work it. I also look at one of the most important things that a person in business must consider: the skills that I need to run the business. In other words, can I do the job?

For instance, if you are going into a baby-sitting business and you don't look at what skills you may need for the job, you could be in big trouble. If you need to change a diaper and you don't know how, what are you going to do? If you need to warm up a bottle and you don't know how hot to make it, what are you going to do? If before you took on the job, you had looked at the skills, things might be different. You might have learned how to change a diaper and warm up a bottle, or you could have decided to go into a different business. So you see, looking at the big picture is very important.

2. To run some of the businesses in this book, won't I have to work with my parents?

Yes, in many cases, that's true. And for all the businesses you'll need their permission and cooperation. Yes, I know, yich. But don't worry. The skill of working with other people, even parents, is called *human relations*. That skill is covered in this book.

You may also have to work with your older or younger brother or sister. That may be even worse. You must always keep an open mind about the people that you are working with. To help you do this, you can think of the rewards that you will get if your business is successful.

As a person who has to work with his mother constantly, I know how hard it can be. Chee, I hope my mom doesn't read this. Anyway, I have worked with my mom for a long time, and it has begun to smooth itself out. So, I included the things I learned about working with older people, including telephone operators and environmentalists, in this book to give you a head start.

3. Arthur, what's the real secret of business success?

As far as I can tell from doing the research for this book and speaking to many successful entrepreneurs, *the real super secret to success is attitude.* Failure attitudes fail, successful attitudes help you to succeed. You need more than the right attitude; but without it, you can't succeed.

A good attitude shows up right away in what you call yourself and even in what you name your business.

It's all in the presentation. When you create a name for the work you do, like waste management consultant, you will look like a real expert. People may be more inclined to use your services, instead of somebody else's, if you identify for them, and they understand, exactly what you do. This could be the difference between a successful business and a bad business.

THE LAST WORD

Before you read this book, you should tell your parents what you are planning. This is very important. If you end up doing something your parents don't like, you might get in trouble. Make your parental units your partners. Good luck, and enjoy the book.

Letter to Mom and Dad

Dear Parents,

Here's the title of a book that would sell a billion copies: *The Ultimate, Once-in-a-Lifetime Secret for Making Your Kids Successful.* There, I said it. The *success* word. In the past two years, my son Arthur, who turned thirteen in 1995, and I have toured the country with our book *The Totally Awesome Money Book For Kids (and Their Parents)*. Every place we went, Arthur was interviewed as a financial expert. Everything from his opinion on the stock market to the London Gold Exchange was of interest to the public and the press.

Donahue called him the next generation of talk show hosts, Oprah put him on a panel of experts, and Jay Leno had him invest $1,000 for the *Tonight Show.*

As for me, folks wanted to know only one thing. They said it in a hundred different ways, but they all meant it the same way: "How did Arthur learn so much about money?" "How did he get so money-smart?" "How can I best teach my kids to be smarter than I am about money so they won't go through what I go through?" Some said it right out. "I'd like my kids to be successful on their own when they grow up. How can I help them?"

At first, I shied away from these questions simply because I didn't think I knew the answer. I'm not a teacher or a child psychologist. I'm just another busy parent, like you. Sometimes I feel guilty about how I handle things. Sometimes I feel proud. And sometimes I give up and let my husband handle the mess. So, what do I know?

Well, there is one thing I know—my own field. I am a lawyer, a financial expert, and even sold stocks and insurance (but don't hold that against me). In the past several years my career has turned to financial journalism and writing. I have written seventeen books on personal finance, I publish "Wealthbuilder," a fast growing newsletter, and host a radio talk show featuring call-in questions on law and money. So, it makes sense that Arthur is aware of financial matters and how to write and speak about them. My work gave me the capacity to help him with both "Totally Awesome" books when he needed it.

Still, all this doesn't account for his mastery over the subject. More important, nor does it account for his success in business life. As a business person and advisor to business for many years, I can attest that knowing what to do and doing it are two very different things. Time after time, I've watched people with good business ideas flounder, and blame everyone for their failure. "Other people have all the luck," "He was born rich," "She married a wealthy husband," "If I only had what they had, I would be a success." You've heard it all before.

I prefer to believe that we make our own luck. That means we have total control over our own success. But, how did Arthur figure that out so soon? Frankly, I didn't know.

Yet, time after time, I was asked by parents for advice, especially when Arthur would lecture at schools or appear on kids' television shows. Many educators, including a few very impressed principals, persuaded me to think hard about what I did to encourage and help Arthur. Since I had been asked by others to "concentrate on my parenting approach," I concentrated. It finally came to me, not because of Arthur, but because of my then two-year-old Rose Phoebe.

When I finally realized the "ultimate secret," it was so simple that I couldn't stretch it out to book length. So, I'll share it with you in a few paragraphs.

It was the cold winter of 1994, and our family went to a restaurant for dinner. Rosie took off her coat, handed it to the proprietor, helped the waiter bring over a high chair, got into it herself, and ordered soup and rice. The restaurant patrons were stunned at the capability of this little girl. I was not impressed. After all, I can do all that, so what's the big deal!

The dinner was the breakthrough. I realized that I expect a lot from my kids because I have extreme respect for them. They are a little short to handle certain things, but they can do a whole lot more than grown-ups think.

The key, I realized, is to constantly give them situations they can master. It snowballs. One positive experience leads to another; one successful endeavor brings on a second, until they have unshakable confidence. Little by little, in bits, they learn.

For example, teaching my children about the buck starts and stops with me. So, I include Arthur in many financial discussions, both about our own family and about money in general. I do not shield him. When we have problems he knows it. So, he has learned that business and financial problems come and go. As a result, he doesn't get too shook up when he has to face one in his own life.

Every time I allow Arthur to handle something, big or small, it reinforces his mastery of life's situations. If I need to fly for a business trip I can make the reservation myself. But, once in a while I ask him to do it. He's learned all about airlines, schedules, and about talking to business people that way.

If he needs to buy supplies for his own business he knows how to find suppliers, because I have shown him the value of trade journals and how people advertise in phone books and newspapers.

And so, when Arthur was about to do this second book teaching kids about business, I was determined to infuse it with my brilliant analysis of how parents can help their children master situations. I was prepared to do that, but I didn't.

After Arthur finished the manuscript, there was nothing left to say. It turns out that the essence of this book if, as Arthur would say, you have the "big picture," is not money or even business. It is mastery of the situation— how to make a telephone call, how to find the right person, how to bargain and negotiate.

In Arthur's words, I hear my own training and my husband's input read back to me, but funnier and more charming. I personally giggled through the whole manuscript. "Speak up." "Don't be intimidated." "Know what your time is worth, and ask to be paid." He had the drill sergeant in me down pat.

The part I like best is the utter confidence that Arthur has—and he's an insider and should know—that any kid can do anything. "Read the water meter." "Write up a contract." "Call an energy expert." "Fix the plumbing." Who are we to suggest they can't do it? We should be there to help them through.

So, better than I ever could, Arthur has revealed the one and only true secret to teaching your children to be a success: *Believe in them.* Teach mastery over a hundred little tasks. The big stuff they'll do themselves.

But, there is one little thing of which I must warn you.Of the twenty businesses described in this book, ten were inspired by Arthur's idea that kids can make money stopping waste in the home. He'll tell you more about it. But it was my comment that started the whole thing.

Arthur does his own research and tests lots of stuff out himself. I'm a nervous type and didn't want him working for strangers, staying in folks' homes alone. It's kind of scary out there these days; safety before revenue. So, he figured that it would be just as good to learn business right at home. Like most kids, he's also a staunch environmentalist and frowns upon the yuppie-style waste that sometimes reigned in our home. (We have subsequently reformed.)

"Doing well by doing good" is a phrase he hears a lot from me. So, he took me up on it to become our own family's waste management consultant. And here's the warning: You are the target market of some of the businesses outlined in this book. You are the customer. Your participation is required in many ways. You will have to:

❏ Make demands
❏ Complain if you don't like the service
❏ Sign contracts
❏ Share necessary information
❏ Pay on time

But you will also save a lot of money! I'm not the type that believes you can make a fortune saving soap ends. And I never met a coupon I had time to cut. But let me tell you this waste management stuff is a powerful savings tool. And what's best, I didn't have to spend a penny's worth of time except to be a good customer and a good sport about changing my terrible wasteful habits, at least some of them.

Now, I can't wait to give the answer to the questions I'll be asked on our next book tour. "How does Arthur know so much about business?" "Well," I'll say, "I taught him everything he knows."

INTRODUCTION

How to Use This Book

This is a really easy book to read; but to use it right, you need to do two things: First, you need to take notes on the parts that apply to you and the ways you plan to make money. Second, you need to do your own thinking to make the businesses described in the book work for you.

The book begins with a review of business in general—how it works and what it's really all about. This is useful even if you are not yet ready to start your own business.

Next, a number of special skills, like using the telephone correctly to get information, negotiating, and speaking up for what you want, are discussed. These skills are needed not only in business but also in many things you do each day.

Finally, different kinds of businesses are described. Or you can use your skills to start a business you thought of yourself. Each section on a suggested business will tell you how much money you can make, what *capital* (money) you need to start the business, the skills you need, and the steps to take to do the work. This is how the section is set up:

NAME OF EACH BUSINESS

The Big Picture:
A description of the business itself.

$–$$$$:

The amount of money you stand to make if you start the business. A single dollar sign means the least amount of money you can make; four dollar signs means the most.

Kid's Capital:

Capital is the amount you invest, spend, or in other ways put into a business to make money. Most of the time, kid's capital will be time only, not money. But some things, like garage sales, also need paid-for advertising. The best businesses are "low in capital" (do not need much money to start or run), "not labor-intensive"(do not need much time to start or run), "cost-effective" (for the capital that you put up, you get a profit that is worth it to you).

Skills:

This tells you what you need to be good at in order to do the job well and make it easy on yourself.

Steps to Success:

This gives you the exact steps you must take to make or to save money.

SKILLS ARE REALLY WHAT THIS BOOK IS ALL ABOUT

Once you have chosen your favorite business, you'll need the skills to do a good job. The skills are explained with forms, charts, and ideas to help you make calls, write letters, and even negotiate deals.

I kid-tested every one of them myself, and they work. For example, I used to feel shy about making phone calls, but I overcame it by following my own advice. The more I did it, the more comfortable I got.

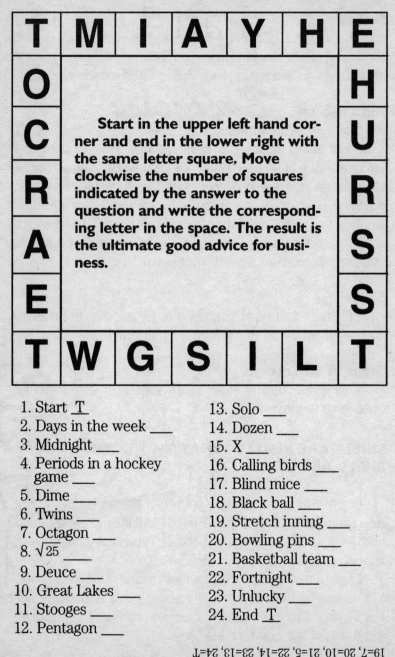

T	M	I	A	Y	H	E
O						H
C						U
R						R
A						S
E						S
T	W	G	S	I	L	T

Start in the upper left hand corner and end in the lower right with the same letter square. Move clockwise the number of squares indicated by the answer to the question and write the corresponding letter in the space. The result is the ultimate good advice for business.

1. Start T
2. Days in the week ___
3. Midnight ___
4. Periods in a hockey game ___
5. Dime ___
6. Twins ___
7. Octagon ___
8. $\sqrt{25}$ ___
9. Deuce ___
10. Great Lakes ___
11. Stooges ___
12. Pentagon ___
13. Solo ___
14. Dozen ___
15. X ___
16. Calling birds ___
17. Blind mice ___
18. Black ball ___
19. Stretch inning ___
20. Bowling pins ___
21. Basketball team ___
22. Fortnight ___
23. Unlucky ___
24. End T

Part 1

Business:

THE BIG PICTURE

1

An Eye for Business

"Why didn't I think of that?"

What is business anyway? The dictionary didn't do me that much good. It said: "an occupation, profession, or trade: *His business is poultry farming*" *(The Random House Dictionary of the English Language,* Second Edition Unabridged*)*.

But business is really a lot of different things. When most people think of business, they think of companies making money. A company is a thing, an *entity*. Different businesses are set up (structured) in different ways. So, just like there are different kinds of people in this world, there are different kinds of business entities. In Chapter 2, you will read about many of them and what they can mean for your business.

So, one answer to "What is business?" is that it is a legal entity structured to carry on a trade, service, or production of goods. The entity has its own name, way of doing things, and some say even a personality.

A business engaged in *trade* is one whose purpose is selling something. It could be a store like Toys "R" Us or a car dealership. These business are in the retail trade. They sell directly to us. We are the consumers.

Another type of trade or selling business is called *supplying.* Suppliers sell to retailers. For example, Mattel and Nintendo sell to Toys "R" Us.

A service business sells help, not things. For example, hairdressers, lawyers, doctors, and car mechanics sell their services to you, the consumer.

A producer of goods manufactures things that are used by trade or service businesses. For example, Schwinn makes the bikes. The bike retail stores sell them.

As you will see in Chapter 3, the trend today is to have businesses do all three: sell, service, and manufacture. A good example is the Warner Bros. stores in the malls. They sell retail (to us); they manufacture the products that go into the stores, and their service center handles the defects and the complaints.

Notice how you knew the names of most of the businesses I just mentioned? Well, that's because businesses have their own identifiable names and unique ways, like I said before, of doing things.

Saturn cars advertise a friendly, homey personality. Ben & Jerry's ice cream advertises a laid-back personality. And the Body Shop cosmetics advertise an environmentally-conscious personality.

Just because they advertise, it doesn't mean the company is run that way. But I read at least a dozen articles about those companies, and the reporters seem to think they are true to their image.

That brings me to another aspect of "What is business?" Business is an idea in the minds of the people who create and start it. That's why it is exciting.

Who was the first person to do business, I wonder? Maybe a caveman who was weak and couldn't find his own food but knew where the animals were. Maybe he offered to tell where the animals were in return for a portion of the hunter's food. Funny to think that business could have started with weakness, but it's probably true. After all, if we could all do everything for ourselves, all the time, we wouldn't need help from others. When others help us and get something in return, they are in business! I don't want all the business parents out there getting mad because I think business started with a caveman who had needs to fill. I love that caveman because he didn't just give up. He took his strengths and a good idea and started a business.

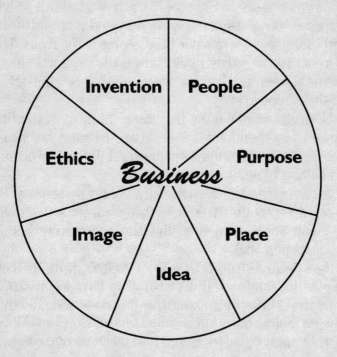

That's an important point. A business must start with a good idea that helps you and others. In Chapter 3, you'll read about ideas, like manufacturing and retailing, that make a business great. They are called the *business purpose*.

When some people think of a business, they think of a place. My great-grandmother, a woman who worked many years before women in general worked, used to say, "I'm going to business." To her, the store where she sold jewelry was business itself.

Today, designing office buildings, plants that manufacture goods, industrial parks, and office space is itself a business, and very important to all other businesses. After all, our caveman needed a convenient rock where hunters could find him. In Chapter 4, you will read about places of business.

The most modern business is the home office using the *information superhighway* (computers and telecommunications). Back to the cave!

For me, the most important answer to "What is business?" is people. Without people, there is no business; and if robots could run a business by themselves, there would be no purpose to it anyway.

Business is all the people who work to make it run. That includes the owners of the business, the secretaries, the management at all levels, and lots more. In Chapter 5, you will learn about the people who work in businesses.

At the end of this book you will be able to take on the role of a special type of worker: the consultant.

We know that businesses have a body (a legal entity), a personality (an image), a goal (business purpose), and a heart (its people). But does business have a conscience?

Does business know right from wrong? Today, the answer to this question is called *business ethics.* I'll cover it in Chapter 6, before we go into business ourselves.

2

The Body of a Business:
Corporations,
Partnerships, and
Sole Proprietorships

Businesses have their own separate names; they file their own tax returns; they even have their own addresses. My mom says a business can live on even after the owner of a business dies. Spooky!

The first car company, Ford Motor, is one example. It was started by Henry Ford before 1910 and is still going strong. But, you don't have to look to the past to find examples of businesses that live on after their founder is gone.

Just by watching television you can see how businesses try to live on. Watch the new Orville Redenbacher popcorn ads. You'll see his grandson dressed just like him, groomed to take over the company. The chicken man, Frank Perdue, is on T.V. with his son Jim. Jim now puts his name on the money back guarantee for each chicken. The ad says he's even tougher than his father. Daughters, too, like Marcy Sym of the famous discount clothing stores Syms, are in on the act. In the Sym's ads, Marcy looks at the camera, just like her father did, and assures us that an educated customer is her best customer. Those companies are all preparing to hand over the helm to the next generation of business people.

A business has a life of its own because it is set up in special ways and registered, usually under government regulations. There are many types of business entities, and more types are being created. Last year there was a conference between the United States and Japan to structure a new type of business entity that could work in outer space.

But today, the three most common types of business entities are: the corporation, the partnership, and the sole proprietorship.

CORPORATIONS

A *corporation* is a business entity in which stocks are issued. The holders of those stocks are the true owners of the corporation. So, *stocks* are shares in a corporation. If you owned all the shares, you would own the whole corporation—its inventory, profits, leases, everything it had. When only a few people own all the shares in a corporation and the shares can't be sold to just anyone else (*restricted shares*) it's called a *closed corporation*. Many family-owned businesses are like that. In T*he Totally Awesome Money Book For Kids (and Their Parents),* you read about a different kind of corporation, a *public corporation,* like Pepsico, McDonald's, Mattel, Toys "R" Us, and hundreds more. It sells shares to the public. If you own a share, you are part owner of the corporation.

To form a corporation, people must have a business idea or purpose. They must put it in writing and file a business certificate in the state where they have a business home. That is called their *state of incorporation.* Once the certificate is accepted, the company is alive! It gets a registered name and applies for a tax identification number (that's a lot like your Social Security number). With it, the corporation can open bank accounts, sign contracts, and do just about everything adult people can do.

Of course, the corporation needs real people to think for it and actually sign its name. They are called its *officers* and *directors.* Some small companies have only one person as an officer and director. Like my mom. She says she wears many hats. She is the president, vice president, treasurer, secretary, and all the other officers and directors of her company. The good part is that when she calls a meeting, everybody arrives on time.

Large corporations, the type you buy shares in, usually have many officers and directors. The CEO (chief executive officer) has one of the most powerful and best-paid jobs in the world. A CEO runs the entire company, does the hiring, and makes the business decisions. But the CEO may not own the corporation; only the shareholders do. Another powerful corporate person is the CFO (chief financial officer). He or she handles the money for the corporation. The CEO and the CFO are still only employees of the company, and therefore, of the shareholders. They get a salary for their work. Sometimes, as part of their compensation they get shares of stock in the company, so they are shareholders, too. So, even a high-paid CEO or CFO works for you if you have a share in a company.

PARTNERSHIPS

Another type of legal entity is the *partnership,* in which two or more people are the owners. No shares are issued. To be an owner, you must make a deal, usually, but not always, with a written contract.

People become partners for many reasons. They may be in the same family and want to work together. They may need to hire someone and can't afford it, so they share the business with someone else. Or they may find someone with lots to offer that is compatible with what they have to offer.

For example, let's say the caveman who knows where to find the food notices that one hunter brings back more than the rest. He says, "Let's be partners. I'll tell you where the food is, you catch it, and we'll sell it to the other cavemen." "Why should we do that?" says the hunter, "What's in it for us?" "Well," says the caveman, "we don't have time to gather fruits and berries. We could exchange meat for fruits and berries and have both that way." "Swell idea," says the hunter, "Let's be partners."

My mom told me not to make partnership arrangements sound too easy. It's hard to find good people to work with that you like. Also, you really must know how to be fair and to share the labor and the profits so each person is happy. That's why most partnerships have a partnership agreement that spells out the rules the partners will abide by.

Many of the businesses in this book can be structured as a partnership with one of your friends. Write up an agreement that includes:

❏ Who does what
❏ Who gets what
❏ How the profits and other stuff the business owns are to be divided if you go out of business

If one of you gives money to the business to buy supplies and the other gives extra time and works more, make sure the way you divvy things up is fair. What is fair? Every partner has a different view. That's one place Skill 6, negotiating, will come in handy.

Today, most partnerships are used for medium-size companies and by doctors, lawyers, and other professionals.

SOLE PROPRIETORSHIPS

A *sole proprietorship* is the easiest of all business entities to start. One (sole) person (proprietor) owns and runs everything. The proprietor may hire employees, but only she or he owns the business. Usually, these are the smallest companies in terms of moneymaking, but not always. As kids, we will probably be sole proprietors. Many sole proprietorships grow and become partnerships with one or more partners. Others incorporate and sell shares.

Some of these corporations *go public,* begin to sell on the stock exchange, and you can buy stock in them. A good example of this is the Celestial Seasonings Company, which began with a sole proprietor picking herbs to make tea. Another example is Weight Watchers, which began with one woman holding meetings in her living room to help her friends lose weight.

My mom was one of the lawyers for Weight Watchers and she also met the owners of Celestial Seasonings on a few television shows where they both talked about business. My mom says that they made it big for lots of reasons that all came together. First, they picked businesses that people really wanted to use. Herbal teas were just right for the health-conscious baby boomers. Diets are always important businesses in overweight America. But, there was more to it than that.

Each company was started by someone who really believed in the business and was passionate about it. Passion is not my word, it's my mom's. But, I'm beginning to understand that it means that they really felt what they were doing was good for everyone, fun to do, and helpful to the world. They were willing to work very hard because of this passion.

I chose my own business because I love the game Magic the Gathering. When I play in tournaments I get to go to colleges, which I enjoy very much. So, I feel happy even when I am doing the drudge work of putting the cards in little plastic cases for resale. It's o.k., because the whole thing is interesting to me.

Some people say that business is what makes the United States great. They say that it's a big reason people come from all over the world to live here. I agree. But I also think it's fun to own your own business. It's creative, like painting a picture or writing a song.

Which brings us to the "business idea."

3

"You can go a long way with the right idea!"

The Mind of a Business: Business Purpose and Idea

Just because there is a piece of paper, like a certificate of incorporation or a partnership agreement, doesn't mean you have a business. You need an idea that lives, too, a purpose to what you are doing and for which you hope to get money. All businesses can be divided up by their purpose. If the purpose is a good one and the idea behind it is smart, you will probably have a successful business. In fact, the mind of the business is much more important than the body. With a good purpose and idea, you will probably make money whether you have a corporation, a partnership, or a sole proprietorship.

Here are some of the top business purposes:

❏ Gathering raw materials (mining for metals, drilling for gas, cutting lumber) to be used in manufacturing
❏ Supplying (selling raw materials to the manufacturers)
❏ Manufacturing (making things that people need)
❏ Wholesaling (selling manufactured goods to the retailers)
❏ Retailing (selling manufactured goods to the public)
❏ Consulting (advising other people or businesses about how to do any part of their business better)

❏ Servicing (providing any kind of service, such as legal, secretarial, cleaning, moving, to people or businesses)
❏ Telecommunication (providing electronic means of talking to and getting messages across to companies and people)
❏ Construction (building homes, roads, bridges, and all types of buildings)

Notice something interesting about these business purposes? Doctors and cleaning services are lumped together; manufacturing airplanes and blue jeans are in the same category. Purposes may be the same in small and big business, in businesses that take lots of skill and those that don't. Businesses with the same purpose can look very different. For example, when I think of manufacturing airplanes, I think of my trip to Seattle to visit Boeing. I lived in Manhattan; and every day, I was practically run over by a garment center guy pushing a rack of clothes down Seventh Avenue. But both businesses are manufacturing.

Here are some businesses. In which category do you think each falls?

___a. Singer
___b. Automobile production
___c. Timber cutting
___d. House building
___e. Gold mining
___f. Telephone service
___g. Soda bottling

Answers: a. Servicing b. Manufacturing c. Raw materials d. Construction e. Raw materials f. Telecommunication g. Wholesaling

Today, they say we are in a postindustrial society. I think that means that all the categories of businesses (industries) have already cropped up, and now we are going beyond it to a world where information gathering will be our most important business purpose. But, it wasn't always like that.

Only a hundred years ago, we were still in a time called the *Industrial Revolution.* People were trying to invent machines that helped manufacture stuff. Here are just a few famous inventors and their dream machines:

1794: Eli Whitney, the cotton gin
1831: Cyrus McCormick, the reaper
1879: Thomas A. Edison, the electric lightbulb

Today, our inventors make new microchips and better semiconductors. Cool.

One thing we do know, no matter how advanced business gets, is that all businesses need the other businesses in the other categories. Just as we depend on each other, most businesses can't get along without each other, either.

Take another look at page 22; you'll see that by definition, business can have three purposes: trade, service, and manufacturing. Trade is selling; service is help; and manufacturing is making things. As you can see, the sellers need the manufacturers or they would have nothing to sell. The manufacturers need the traders or no one will sell their goods. The service people either repair the goods if something goes wrong or provide other services that

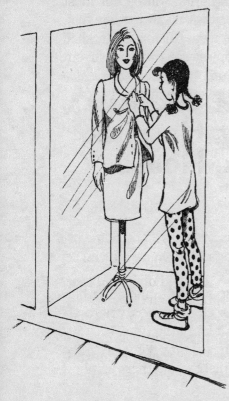

can only be done through human effort, like fixing the plumbing or telling jokes.

So, the:

❑ Service business (shop-window designer) needs the

❑ Retailer (shop owner), who needs the

❑ Wholesaler (seller of goods), who needs the

❑ Manufacturer (maker of goods), who needs the

❑ Supplier of raw materials (cotton merchant), who needs the

❑ Raw materials (cotton).

And they all use tele-communication in order to make their work easier.

That's the business circle of interdependency.

Write down some of your great business ideas. In which categories do they fall? Which other businesses will you need to make yours work?

4

The Home of a Business: Office, Factory, Hospital, Industrial Park, House

Of all the aspects of "What is business?" the home of a business is the easiest to understand, because we can see it, at least for now.

Most of us have visited our mother's and/or father's office. Maybe our grandparents', too. This is where the personality of a business shows a lot of the time.

Some offices are huge; others are tiny. Some are full of state-of-the-art high-tech equipment, and others just have a typewriter.

Of course, retail businesses have stores; and whether it's a butcher shop or a big department store, the store is home for the business. But some of the biggest retail businesses have no stores. They sell through catalogues or television shopping networks. Those retail businesses have a home, too, usually an office building that their customers never see.

Until I moved to New Jersey, I had never seen an *industrial park*. One near us has a hotel, a day-care center, and an emergency room, built on lawns that look like golf courses.

Office design is a business in itself that you might want to go into one day.

Not only stores and offices but factories, too, are homes for business. The old-fashioned factories have been replaced by state-of-the-art machinery that helps do work faster and more efficiently. But some of the new machines replace people with robots. That's another part of our post-industrial world. Routine factory jobs are being eliminated in favor of machines doing the work. Some people are out of work that way, and their families are hurt.

Businesses have growing pains just like kids. And those pains can be big.

As you can see, it's hard to talk about something even as simple as a factory without getting into important issues like: Should we slow up manufacturing progress to keep jobs going? It's a big issue. Some call it progress, others call it big business not caring for the little guy. What do you think?

Here's another interesting thing about the place of business: It may be going back to the home. In the 1700s, before the Industrial Revolution, most places of business were on the farm and in the home. When manufacturing began, the new machines, like looms and sewing machines, were operated right in the house. These businesses were called *cottage industries*.

By the 1800s, factories were built. If you go to Washington, D.C., you can visit a building in the Smithsonian Institution that shows you factories and machinery of the Industrial Revolution. They are beautiful and very old-fashioned.

By the 1950s, office buildings, sleek factories, and industrial parks housed a lot of businesses and took up a lot of space. They still do.

But there is another revolution. Because of computers and telecommunication, millions of people are working from home again. Over 9 million at last count are *telecommuting*. They work for a company, but they work at home and communicate through their computers using modems.

I have an example at home. My mom writes a newsletter. She uses a printing company, a company that takes orders, an 800-number company, a Visa/Mastercard company, and a fulfillment house that puts postage on the newsletter and mails it out. She has never seen any of these companies. In fact, they are all in other states. They all communicate by computer. My mom's only equipment is a three-pound computer that she carries in a backpack. So, I guess my mom's place of business is her backpack!

When you select the business you want to start, come back to this chapter and design your ideal business home.

5

The Heart of a Business: People

More than ever, we are learning that people are the heart of business. At first, the owners of businesses believed that the people who worked there were very unimportant. Child labor, low wages, and horrible working conditions were all part of the Industrial Revolution. But things changed. Labor unions, strikes, and even violence are all part of business history. A *labor union* is like a club workers can join in together in order to make their employer deal with them as a group, rather than as individuals. This gives the employees more power. One way to use this power is for everyone to stop working all at once until the employer gives them what they want. When workers stop working, it's called *going on strike.*

There are both state and federal fair labor laws with which business must comply. There are labor-management contracts that can be enforced in the courts and at special hearings called *arbitrations.*

Today, there are different issues about people in business. Those issues are about fair hiring practices so that blacks, woman, older people, and others aren't discriminated against in hiring.

Not everyone agrees on what is fair. Many say that businesses work best when they are run by all types of folks, each bringing new ideas and ways of doing things. Others feel that government and unions have no right to dictate so many rules to business, and that what's good for one group may become unfair to another.

What do you think? Is *affirmative action*—requiring businesses to hire certain people, like blacks and women, who were excluded from working in the past, a good idea or not? Or should all hiring be based on ability to do the job only?

How about allowing U.S. businesses to use workers from other countries that pay their workers only a few pennies an hour and that still put children to work ?

These are hard questions. Talk to your parents about them. When I do, there are always lots of very loud discussions about whether business does best when it's free to do as it likes or whether it needs regulation. My father is a labor lawyer who works with both labor and management. Boy, does he have ideas! Turn off the radio in the car one day, and ask these questions to your mom and dad. Then sit back and watch the fireworks.

No matter what their politics, most people still agree that people are the heart of a business. If you look at the different things that people do in a business, the roles they can play, you can get an idea of what jobs you would like to fill even if you don't have a business of your own.

Here are some ways businesses use their *personnel* (people):

UPPER MANAGEMENT
❏ Officers (president, vice president, treasurer)
❏ Directors

These people make top decisions about the business as a whole: How much will be manufactured, what line of toys will be sold at Christmas, what advertising style will mark the image of the business.

MIDDLE MANAGEMENT
❏ Department heads
❏ Vice presidents (sometimes)

These people carry out the decisions of upper management and make decisions of their own regarding how to get things done. They also supervise the support staff.

SUPPORT STAFF
❏ Secretaries
❏ Receptionists
❏ Administrators
❏ Bookkeepers
❏ Computer operators
❏ Factory workers
❏ And just about anybody else who is not management

As you can imagine, each company is very different when it comes to its workers. In some small businesses, the owner (upper management) does his or her own typing. In other businesses, there may be a very powerful vice president in charge of marketing a product. In other industries, like banking, lots of people are given the title of vice president, but many of them are not in upper management at all.

So, the one thing I learned is not to be fooled by titles on a business card. But even though I say that, most people do care what their title is. They feel better as vice president of interoffice communications than they do as mail room attendant.

Make up fancy names for these jobs:

Teacher _____

Lawyer _____

Janitor _____

Computer operator _____

Author _____

Sanitation worker _____

Nurse

Manicurist

Cook

Assembly-line auto worker

More and more businesses are learning that they do better and are more productive (make more money) when their workers are happy. Today, there is a trend toward flextime for working mothers, stress-release sessions, and gyms in the workplace. Telecommuting is also a big new part of making workers happier.

We've come a long way from sweatshops and child labor. Many other countries in the world have a long way to go to catch up to our standards. We have many faults. But, basically, after reading about working conditions for this book, I am very proud of the United States.

Which brings us to the chapter on the conscience of a business.

6

The Conscience of a Business: Business Ethics

Businesses are a lot like people. They can't just do anything they want. They can't cheat you, pollute rivers, or make medicines that harm you. They are under a lot of regulation, mostly from the federal government.

This is not a book on politics, but it's hard to write about business today without mentioning Washington, D.C. There are vast differences of opinion about how much control the government should have over business. Some say none at all; just let the people stop using a business if they don't like it. Then it will "go out of business." People who feel this way are sometimes called *conservatives*. Others feel that the government is needed to protect us from bad business practices. People who feel this way are sometimes called *liberals*.

The main question that we, as business kids, have to ask ourselves is whether we think a business has an obligation to do the right thing even if it means making less profit. Everyone agrees that the goal of every business is to make more money than it takes to run the operation. If lots more is made, then it's called a *good* business. If only a little more is made, the business is called *marginal*. If it costs more to run than it makes, it will eventually go out of business.

But what if profits can be made by cutting the quality of the raw materials used or importing cheap labor? Does a business have a duty to make less money, maybe pay some of its top people less, or even go out of business instead of cutting corners?

If you think these are tough questions, what about this one? Does a business have the obligation not to manufacture or sell something the public wants because it's no good for the public? Examples of this are cigarettes and alcohol. What about animal testing for medical research? Some people think it's wrong. Others think it's okay because it saves human lives.

I love the idea of going into business; and if you got this far into the book, you probably do, too. Here's the way I see it: Government regulates business too much. Paperwork and taxes can stop a lot of good businesses before they start. But the reason this has happened is that businesses were only out for profit and didn't show a conscience. We are a new generation of business people. We know better. Maybe if we are better, no one will have to tell us what to do.

Part 2:

Business Skills:

EVERYDAY THINGS YOU HAVE TO KNOW TO RUN YOUR BUSINESS

7

"You can really go far if you let your voice be heard."

Skill 1: Speaking Up

WHY DON'T MOST PEOPLE SPEAK UP?

1. People don't think that it's worth the effort.
2. People don't know how or where to complain.
3. People don't believe that it will do any good.
4. People are afraid that they will get yelled at or laughed at when they speak up. They don't want to get their feelings hurt.

All these reasons that people are afraid of speaking up are, for the most part, mistaken. It is worth the effort; it will do good; and it's easy to learn how and whom to talk to.

HOW TO SPEAK UP

Complaining is not that hard. First, you need a problem. If you don't have a real need, then you *will* get laughed at or ignored.

But when you *do* have a real problem, you should not be afraid to speak up. This is how to do it: If it is something simple, like you feel that you were not charged the right price at the supermarket, you can start out with: "Excuse me, I believe that you have not charged me the price that it says on the ticket." That will usually work. If it is something that is more complicated, like a problem with your phone bill, you might want to have some proof, like showing the incorrect bill. Most of the time, people don't get what they want because they don't know how to get it. When you call up to complain, always have a solution and a date by which you want results.

If you call for a favor, like a price break, be ready to negotiate in order to get what you want.

WHY SPEAK UP?

You should always speak up because there's a good chance that you will get results and no chance if you don't. It's not just to make someone feel bad or get them in trouble. That's a type of complaining that doesn't work. But result-style complaining does. Sometimes you can change the world by complaining.

If you are especially good at speaking up, you can join a *lobby group*. A lobby group is a group of people who speak to people high in our government about a certain issue that they have a strong opinion about.

WHERE TO SPEAK UP (WHOM TO TALK TO)

If you are speaking up about something, you need to make sure you talk to someone who can really help you, not a receptionist or someone in the wrong department. Usually, when you have a problem, you should speak to the person in charge of the company or business that did you wrong. Don't complain to a friend, because a friend can't do anything about it. Find the person with the most power.

WHEN TO SPEAK UP

You should speak up when you have a problem with service, prices, or because of any other injustice. Complain immediately; don't let the complaint get old. The best time to complain is during the week (but not on a Friday).

There are two good times to call during the day. One good time is first thing in the morning; the other good time is right after the people you are going to complain to get back from their lunch break.

WHAT IF YOU DON'T GET RESULTS?

If you don't get results the first time that you complain, you should try again. You will probably get results the second time. There are other things that you can do if you can't get results just by calling the company that you are having the problem with. There are many places that can help you: the Better Business Bureau, Call for Action, your local radio station, and even your congressperson. You can also contact government agencies. See the list in *The Great American Gripe Book,* by Matthew Lesko (Kensington, Md.: Information USA, Inc., 1991).

Don't forget to put everything in writing. As soon as you speak to someone get a letter out that confirms either the offer to help or the refusal. Send it to the person you spoke to and send a copy to his or her boss. Be sure to give a date by which you want results.

Businesses in This Book That May Include Speaking Up

These include businesses that involve checking bills sent to your parents, for example, telephone and electric bills. These are called utility bills and are sometimes wrong. The best place to call is the state utilities commission. But first look on the bill, because many of them may actually have a complaint telephone number on them.

" *Almost 70 percent of people with consumer problems don't complain. Too bad, because 40 percent of people who took action were satisfied with the results. (See the Gripe Book)*" —Responsible Rhoda

"Everyone needs a budget in business."

8

Skill 2: Making Business Budgets

WHAT IS A BUSINESS BUDGET?

A *business budget* is a way of figuring out if you are making or losing money in your business. A budget is a must if you are in business.

BUDGET VERSUS CASH FLOW

Cash flow is the "time" when you receive and spend money. Sometimes you spend and get paid at the same time, sometimes at different times. If you have to spend before the money comes in, you have a *cash flow problem.*

When you make a business budget, you must take cash flow into account. Even if you make more money each month than you spend, you still may get a bill that you cannot pay on time because your cash has not come in yet. You should always make sure that you have cash so that you can pay a bill anytime it may come in.

HOW TO MAKE A BUDGET

Budgeting is not that hard after you do it a few times. In general, this is how you make a budget: Write down all the things that you make money (*income*) from. Then

Cash Flow			
Income:		**Expenses:**	
1. Farm Sale, May 30	$10.00	1. Plastic Bags, June 1	$7.00
2. Farm Sale, June 5	$10.00	2. Ribbons, June 1	$3.00
3. Farm Sale, July 5	$10.00	3. Worms, June 6	$4.00
Total	$30.00	**Total**	$14.00

write down how much money you make from each item. Next, total up the money that you make. The next step is to do the same thing with your expenses. Finally, subtract the expenses from the income. If there is money left over, you are doing very well. If the result is zero, you have a balanced budget. But if the expenses are greater than the income, you are in trouble and have to cut down the spending or increase the income.

ARTHUR'S TOTALLY AWESOME HOBBY/BUSINESS

A few months ago I started to play a game called Magic the Gathering. It is a card game that is sort of like Dungeons and Dragons. In the last few months, this game has gotten very popular. The company that makes this game did not make enough cards to meet the demand of the stores. A lot of kids like this game, and the stores can't get enough cards to sell to them. So, I thought that I could make money by selling some of my cards to the local card store in my town. What I do is, I open packs and the cards that I want, I keep. The cards that I don't want, I give to the card store and they sell them for me. The store gets 30 percent of whatever they sell, and I get 70 percent of what they sell. The cards that they don't sell I get back to keep.

The purpose of my business is being a supplier. Here is a timesheet, a profit/loss statement, an income sheet, and an expense sheet that relates to my business.

EXPENSE SHEET—WEEKLY
Packs $35.00
Transportation $.45
Packaging $10.00
Total Cost $45.45

INCOME SHEET—WEEKLY
Income from store (Average) $50.00 (70%)
Inventory $50.00 ———————————
Total $100.00

PROFIT/LOSS STATEMENTS—WEEKLY
Income Per Week $100.00
Expenses Per Week $45.45 ———————
Profit $54.55

TIMESHEET—WEEKLY
Hours worked per day:
1 hour, 7 days a week = 7 hours a week
Profit = $54.55
Profit divided by hours worked = $\frac{(54.55)}{(7)}$ = $7.79

I make $7.79 an hour

WORKING WITH A BUSINESS BUDGET

A business budget is exactly the same as a regular budget, but it tells you the income you get only from the business and the money you spend (*expenses*) only for that business. Here's my budget for an old business of mine, Arthur's Good Garbage. I sold compost as described in Business 6:

Arthur's Business Budget: May 30 to August 15				

EXPENSES:

Item	Cost			
Plastic bags	$7.00			
Ribbons	$3.00		**Total Income:**	$30.00
Worms	$4.00		**Total Costs**	$14.00
Total:	$14.00		**Profit over 6 weeks**	$16.00

INCOME

Sale	May 30	$10.00
Sale	May 30	$10.00
Sale	May 30	$10.00
Total:		$30.00

WHY SHOULD YOU BUDGET?

You should budget because if you do, you will know if you have a good business or a bad business. When you budget, you should always make sure that you are writing the right numbers down; otherwise, you think that your business is doing badly when it's really doing well. Or you might think that your business is doing well when in reality it's not doing well.

If you don't budget you might:

❏ Work without making money
❏ Never realize how good your business is and not expand
❏ Not know how to cut costs
❏ Not know if you are charging enough for your work

Here is a sample budget for you to fill out. Try it before you start a business. It will help you decide if it's a good one.

Income:

allowance:	$
gifts:	$
business income:	$
odd jobs:	$
other income:	$
Total Income:	$

Expenses:

business expenses:	$
things you want to spend on:	$
lunch:	$
charity:	$
Total Expenses:	$

Total Income:	$
minus Total Expenses:	$
Equals:	$

How are you doing?
❏ I have money to spare. I'm doing great.
❏ I need to spend less.
❏ I'm balanced.

DON'T BE AFRAID OF A BUDGET

Some people don't budget because they are afraid that a budget will limit them and keep them from getting what they want. It's not true. Budgets, business or personal, are the only way to set financial goals and achieve them.

One of the biggest reasons people go out of business is that they don't have enough capital to start or keep up a business. If they made a budget to begin with, they would know what they were in for before they started. This is called a *preliminary budget*. Do one now for a business that interests you.

Here's some math stuff that will help you to make a budget.

Averages

To find the average of something, you have to add all the numbers together, then divide the total sum by the number of numbers you added together. For example, suppose that you made $15 one week, $20 the next week, and $18 the third week, and you wanted to find out the average of your earnings for those weeks. First, you add all of your earnings together. You will get a total of $53. You then divide that total by 3 because you added 3 numbers together to get $53. You then get $17.66. That is the average amount of money you made per week.

Percentages

To find a percentage of something, you have to divide the second number by the first number. For example, suppose you had 80 baseball cards and 10 of them were Yankee cards and you wanted to find out what percentage of your cards were Yankee cards. You would have to divide 10 by 80. You would get 0.13. Since all percentages are based on 100, 0.13 is 13 percent of 100. So, 13 percent of your cards are Yankee cards.

> "You might need a Rolodex, file folders, envelopes, and labels."

Skill 3:
Record Keeping and Filing

THE IMPORTANCE OF RECORDS

Records are the life of your business. Without them, you don't know what you have to do next and you can't keep track of what you have already done for your business. Records serve many purposes. They tell you:

1. What people owe you (accounts receivable)
2. What people paid you already (income)
3. What you owe others (accounts payable)
4. What you paid others (expenses)
5. Business budget
6. Names and addresses of suppliers
7. Names and addresses of customers

Let's say that you were going into the garage sale business. Here is a list of records that you might keep besides the records I just listed:

1. What you have sold
2. How much you sold those items for
3. How many people came to your sale
4. How many pieces of merchandise you brought to the sale and didn't sell

PROFIT AND LOSS RECORDS

A *profit and loss* record is the last part of your business budget. Just take the total income and subtract the total expenses. You get your profit or loss for the month. After about three months, you can tell how your business is doing. If after a while there is a big change, you may be doing something different that is causing the change. It could be good (a bigger profit) or bad (a smaller profit or a loss). The statement keeps you alert to business change so you can do more of the good stuff and fix the bad.

TIME SHEETS

I learned about *time sheets* from my parents, who are both lawyers. Lawyers are mostly paid for their time at an hourly rate. They have to prove to their clients how much time they spent on a case so they can get paid. As waste consultants, we may be paid by the hour, too, and need to keep time records. But mostly we will be paid with a cut, a part of the money saved. Still, time records are very important for a consultant. We will always be using our time as our capital. Keep records of how much time you spend each day at your business:

Date:_____ · Job ._____· Hours _____

_____   _____   _____

_____   _____   _____

By knowing how much money you made in your business through the profit and loss records, you can figure out how much you earned per hour. Just divide the profit for the month by the time for the month:

$$\frac{\text{Profit}}{\text{Time}} = \frac{\$20.00}{4 \text{ hours}} = \$5.00 \text{ per hour}$$

You can then compare what you earned with something that pays strictly by the hour, like baby-sitting. In most places, the minimum wage for grown-ups is $4.50 per hour. How is your business doing compared with the minimum wage?

FILING

After you know what records you need, you must set up a *filing system*. I like to use envelopes because papers fall out of files that are open. Files with tie strings are big and expensive. So, I use 8½-by-11 envelopes that close with a metal fastener. I just write the date and the name of the paper I put in. I write this information down on a top sheet that I keep in the envelope. That's all I do. I keep the envelopes in my desk drawer in alphabetical order. Here's a list before and after it's been alphabetized:

List of files	List Alphabetized
Smith	Carson
Jones	Jackson
Samson	Jones
Jackson	Samson
Carson	Smith

How to Alphabetize

To alphabetize, you just take the first letter of the file. *A* comes before *B*, and so on. If the files have the same first letter, just go to the next letter. Choose the system that works best for you. But file every day, or else the whole thing gets out of hand and so messy you'll never find anything.

10

Skill 4: Telephoning

DON'T BE INTIMIDATED

When you're on the phone with an adult, do not be afraid to talk. Speak up. If the adult you are talking to giggles or laughs, it's not to make you embarrassed. He's probably just giggling because he is flabbergasted that you are doing this. When you are talking, never feel that the adult that you're talking to is trying to get you off the phone.

SPEAK SLOWLY

Whenever you are talking on the phone, always speak slowly and clearly. You should even do that when you're not on the phone with adults. Always make sure that you don't drop your voice at the end of a sentence or a word. When you speak, always make sure that the adult doesn't have to say "What?" all the time.

WHAT IF THE ADULT DOESN'T WANT TO TALK TO YOU?

If the adult you are trying to reach doesn't want to talk to you, you should say, for instance, that you are trying to help stop waste. Adults will want to talk to you if they know you have a serious purpose and are not wasting their time. It's good to say something nice to them like, "Your job at the telephone company must be pretty interesting," or, "Everyone said that you would have the right information for me."

If the person you want to speak to isn't in her office, or is on vacation, or in a meeting, you should leave a message saying the time that you called, your name, your number, and the reason for your call. Also mention when it would be a good time for them to call you back.

TAKE NOTES

When you talk on the phone about a business matter, you should always have a pencil and paper with you and take notes. When you're on the phone, it's important to take notes in case you forget anything that you talked about during the conversation. Make a note of whom you called, why you called, when you called, and whom you should call next or what you should do next. Write down the  information you got and any numbers you need for the future, and the best time to call them.

ALWAYS FOLLOW UP

Whenever you are making calls about a business matter, you should always make sure that you follow up. After you have talked to somebody, and that person tells you to call someone else for more information, you should always do it. Never leave a job half done.

"My fingers do the walking."

Skill 5:
Using the Telephone Book

ALPHABETIZE THE POSSIBILITIES

When you use a phone book, the things that you look up are in alphabetical order. Alphabetical order is a way of organizing a list; you put the words in order by first letter of the word. Words that start with *A* come before words that start with *B*; words that start with *B* come before words that start with *C*, and so on. *Z* words come last. If two or more words start with the same letter, you should go on to the next letter. So, if you were alphabetizing names, my name, "Arthur," would come after "Adam" because *R* comes after *D*.

LET'S SEE WHAT THE TELEPHONE BOOK CAN DO FOR YOU

Telephone books are amazing things. They can tell you a lot. Here are some of the things you can find in this book: In the white pages, you can find a listing of businesses in your area. In the blue pages, you can find a list of all federal, state, county, and local government offices in your area. The yellow pages can tell you the products and services available in your area. This is where you can look up restaurants, for example. You will also find your local gas, power, and light companies listed in the yellow pages. The green pages have coupons that can help you be a smart consumer.

You can also find a list of zip codes for your state so you can address your business letters properly, and you can also find diagrams of local sports arenas. There are maps showing the location of parks, area attractions, and museums. You can also find the numbers for, and information about, your local theaters.

HOW TO USE THE TELEPHONE BOOK

The two main divisions of the telephone book are the white pages, which list people's names and addresses and businesses' names and addresses in alphabetical order, and the yellow pages, which list businesses by the type of business they do. The types or categories are in alphabetical order.

When you use the yellow pages, you look for what you need by its first letter. Look for the general category first. For instance, if I wanted to find a Chinese restaurant, I would look under R, for "restaurants," not under C for "Chinese." Then, when you find what you need, you get specific. For example, after I find the section on Chinese restaurants under the restaurant category, I can look for the one with the location I need.

Sometimes businesses put ads in the yellow pages that tell about themselves. These ads make it easier to decide what's right for you. In fact, the phone book is a very important way of advertising any business.

There is an index in the back of the book that can help you find the things you need. So, if you are not sure how something is listed, look at the back of the yellow pages. The index lists things under different names to help you.

For example, if you wanted to buy tickets to the ball game, you might look up "Tickets." But nothing is listed.

Look at the index under "Tickets" and you will be told to look up: "Airline Ticket Agencies," "Railroads," "Steamship Agencies," "Travel Agencies," and "Ticket Sales—Entertainment and Sports." Now you can find the ticket information you want under "Ticket Sales—Entertainment and Sports" in the main part of the book.

When you use the white pages, you should look up what you want by the last name of the person or the first word of the name of the business. If there are a few people with the same last name as the person that you are trying to look up, you should look at the first initial.

Everything is alphabetized in the white pages, just like in the yellow pages. After you have found the right name, you will see the telephone number and address, too.

It is very important to use the telephone book. If you call Information (or Directory Assistance) instead of looking up the number, it costs 30 cents a call from most places.

12

"To get what you want, you might have to give something, too."

Skill 6: Negotiating

DEFINITION

Negotiation is the way that you work out a contract. We talk more about contracts in Chapter 13.

KNOW WHAT YOU WANT

When you go in to negotiate a contract, you should always know what you want. Always ask for it flat out. You may get it without a fight. That sometimes happens, but not usually. Most people will not be willing to give you everything that you want. But there are many ways that you can get what you want. Do as much as you can to get it.

LISTEN TO OTHERS

When you are negotiating a contract, you should always know what the other person wants. You need to know because if you don't, you might offer that person something he or she doesn't want. You can learn what that person wants by listening.

FIND SOMETHING YOU HAVE THAT THE PERSON YOU ARE NEGOTIATING WITH CAN USE

If you have a problem negotiating and nobody wants to give anything up, you can offer to give a free service or promise to refer business to the person you are negotiating with. Doing this may help move the negotiation along.

DON'T BE INTIMIDATED

When you are negotiating, never be intimidated by the other person, especially if he or she is an adult. That person may be just as afraid as you are. If you never get intimidated, then you are probably a good negotiator. When you negotiate, you should always hold your ground. Don't give up what you want easily.

13

"I always get it down on paper."

Skill 7: Putting it in Writing

After you negotiate a contract with your parents or anybody that you are doing business with, you should always put your agreement in writing. When you put your agreement in writing, it becomes a contract you can count on. If you disagree with the person who made the contract about what it says, you can always read the contract together. If nothing is in writing, it's the other person's word against yours.

There are many other reasons why you should put your agreements in writing. Here are some of those reasons: If you don't put it in writing, the person might do something that you didn't agree that he should do. Another reason is that you might lose money. If the other person is a boss and gives you less than the original bargain, you can't prove what is really owed to you. But the main reason to have a contract is to avoid misunderstandings and prevent fights.

WHAT TO PUT IN A CONTRACT

There are a few things that you have to put in a written contract. You must put in the names of the people who are involved. You must list the date that the contract was

```
                W.M.C. Contract

DATED:_____

   Gail Goalsetter, from now on called "The
Waste Management Consultant" (WMC) and
Parental Unit, from now on called "The Cus-
tomer," agree as follows:

   1. The WMC will prepare a Water Audit
together with a report and recommendations for
saving money at no initial cost to the cus-
tomer.

   2. The customer will let the WMC look at
the meter, toilets, and all areas necessary
for audit.

   3. The customer will follow at least the
three most important recommendations in the
report.

   4. The WMC will prepare a monthly savings
report using the bills supplied by the cus-
tomer and receive 50 percent of the savings
directly from the customer.

   5. If customer does not do the first three
important recommendations, WMC will receive
the sum of $25.00 for the work done in the
report.

   6. The audit will be completed 60 days from
the signing of this Agreement.
```

Gail Goalsetter   *May 5, 1995*
_____
Waste Management Consultant

Mrs. Jones   *May 5, 1995*
_____
Parental Unit

signed. You must write down what the people involved have to do; that's the thing that is most important. You also have to tell by what dates the people have to do their deeds. Another very important thing that you have to put into your contract is how much the people involved get paid and who will pay.

WHAT TO DO IF THE OTHER PERSON IN YOUR CONTRACT DOESN'T DO WHAT HE OR SHE IS SUPPOSED TO DO

If the other person doesn't do what he or she is supposed to do, you can talk about it and show him or her the contract. If the other person still doesn't do the right thing, you can write a polite business letter insisting that he or she do it.

That's about all kids can do because it's too expensive for us to sue in a court for breach of contract. But what we can do is refuse to work for or do business with that person anymore.

HOW TO CHANGE THE DEAL IF IT DOESN'T WORK

Sometimes, when things are not going well with a deal, if you talk about it, you will find out the problem. For example, if someone is not paying you on time to mow the lawn, he might not like your work, or someone may be sick at home and he forgot. That's why it helps to talk. You or the other person may feel that the original deal was a mistake. Many times, new deals can be worked out.

If the deal doesn't work, you can tell the other party that you don't like the way the company is being run and you want to renegotiate the deal. If you both agree, you should write the word *void* on the old contract. Then you should write up a new contract.

14

Skill 8:
Marketing and Advertising

PICK A TARGET MARKET

A *target market* is a group of people who are just the kind of people that may want to use your product or service. To find your target market, you have to imagine who they are. For instance, if you are pet-sitting, you may want to look for people who are going on vacation and who have pets.

Another way to find a target market is to do a test. Offer your service to people of different age groups and see who buys. Or sell to boys and girls and keep track of how many of each bought. Keeping records of who bought from you is the most important thing that you can do to discover your target market.

Trying to sell to everyone is a lot of work. You make more money faster if you can go right to the people who want you.

One way of marketing is called *direct mail*. You will read about many others later on. With direct mail you send a letter to a person and ask them to buy your product by sending in money. This is a difficult way to market because many people see this as junk mail. So to test the market you must be very careful only to mail to those who are likely to want your product.

Here's the story of a real test done by my mom to find the target audience for her newsletter. Then I'll tell you how I'm going to use what she did for my own business.

My mom bought a list (there are companies that sell lists with names and addresses, usually about $80 per thousand names). She chose one where the people were over the age of 65 and one where people were 35-55 years old. She wants to see if her newsletter appeals to an older or younger target market. Once she knows this, she can make better choices about where to advertise.

This gave me an idea. I wanted to see if I could sell my Magic the Gathering cards directly to kids, instead of only in the store. This would give me another outlet for sale. A direct mail package from a company called Val U Pack came to our home. Maybe you have seen them or something like

them. Stores and other businesses in the neighborhood pay to be included in a mailing and they offer a discount or premium to the customer. A coupon for the offer is included in the pack.

This is an inexpensive way to advertise. But, it's still too expensive for me. So, I asked the pizza store if they would offer a free Magic the Gathering card (which I would provide) to the first 100 kids who ask for it. They said "yes" and agreed to mention this premium in their coupon. I gave them 100 cards free to give away. So, what did I get out of this?

If lots of kids ask for a card then I know that they read the coupons and are interested in what I have to sell. If very few people bother to ask for the freeby, then either kids don't read the coupons or, if they do, they don't care about Magic the Gathering.

If the test is a success I will try to save the money to insert my own mail order coupon in the pack.

WHAT MAKES YOUR TARGET MARKET WANT WHAT YOU HAVE TO OFFER?

People go to different people to do the work that they need done for many reasons. Some may like a good price and not expect the best work. Others don't mind a high price as long as the job is done very well. Still others like the job done quickly. To have a successful business, you have to be able to accommodate your best customers and give them what they want. Once you have customers, take a survey. Find out what they like about your business and keep doing it. Ask them what needs improvement and fix it. Your business will get better and better.

HOW WILL YOU GET YOUR TARGET MARKET TO LISTEN TO YOU?

You must *market* and *advertise* your businesses. No business makes money if no one knows it's there!

WHAT IS MARKETING?

The way to get to the target market is by marketing. *Marketing* is everything a business does to get its target market (customers) to know about it and buy its product or service. This includes finding the target market, taking the surveys, testing the market, and advertising.

WHAT IS ADVERTISING?

Remember, marketing is all the ways that you get people to buy your product, use your services, improve your product, find the right price to charge, and add to your target market. One way of marketing is advertising. *Advertising* is getting across the message about your business.

There are many ways for you to advertise. One way is to pay for radio ads, although those may be too expensive for you. You can also put an ad in the paper. Now, here are some tips for free advertising. Put up signs on telephone poles and bulletin boards in your school, in your town hall, or even in your post office. Another way is to make flyers and pass them out. A *flyer* is a piece of paper that advertises a business. It helps if you make your flyers colorful. A third way is to make business cards. *Business cards* are cards that tell the name of your business, your business telephone number, and your name.

WHAT IS PUBLICITY?

Another popular way of marketing a business is through unpaid advertising called publicity. Instead of choosing a T.V. or radio station or magazine and buying ad time or space, you can get someone on the station or a reporter for the magazine to mention you free. This is called publicity. To accomplish this you must tell them something newsworthy, fun, or different about your company or yourself.

A grand opening with an elephant in the front of a store gets attention and publicity. I get a lot of publicity because

I'm a kid who writes books. You must think of something unique and tell it to those with the power to tell others.

You do this by writing a press release that tells your story. Find the people who can tell the world about you by looking at the pages of newspapers for the names of editors and writers. There is also a book in your library called *Publicity Outlets*. It gives the names, addresses, and phone numbers of journalists and broadcasters who want press releases. I've used it and I can tell you that people in radio, T.V., and journalism move around a lot. So, many times you have to call the station or paper to find the right person.

13-YEAR-OLD BRINGS MAGIC TO OUR TOWN

A new business has arrived in town. The business is run by Arthur Bochner. He is selling cards for a popular game that is taking the country by storm. The game is called Magic the Gathering. The manufacturer, Wizards of the Coast, did not make enough cards to meet the demands of all of the people who play the game. As a result of this, local stores have a shortage of cards. Arthur Bochner is supplying cards to anxious youngsters through the local card store on Main Street. Because of this, the people who live in the area have an ample supply of cards. Bravo!

IMPORTANT POINTS OF A PRESS RELEASE

1. Name of Business
2. How to get the product
3. Where to get the product
4. Date of events (if any)
5. A catchy title
6. Something unique
7. A quote

Don't get discouraged. Even one mention helps your business enormously. A book by Al Parinello called *On the*

Air, published by Career Press, shows you how to get interviewed by radio talk show hosts about your business. Take it from me, stories about kids in business are in demand. Call your local radio station, even if it's a music station with no talk. If you have something interesting to say you could get interviewed. Once I heard a disc jockey called to dedicate a song to the opening of a new company. That was pretty smart.

WHAT IS PROMOTION?

Sometimes you can't think of anything unique about your business and you have to create something to write a press release about. This is called promotion. You can give hats away if they buy your stuff, have a clown at your lemonade stand, get a famous person to appear at an event, or give some of your profits to charity. Now you have something to say in your press release.

WHAT ARE PREMIUMS, SALES, TWO-FOR-ONES, AND SHORT-TIME-ONLYS?

Sometimes you must give your customers more incentive to buy your product or use your services. To do this they need to be offered something extra. There are many ways to go about this. All are part of marketing.

You can give away a pencil with your name on it or other goodies free with every purchase. This is called a *premium.* It's a business all by itself. Every year there are conventions of people in the premium business, with hundreds of booths showing frisbees, caps, yo-yos, and other freebies. Or you can have a sale.

Which is better?

half off	50 percent off
two-for-one	buy-one-get-one-free

Of course, the first two are the same as each other and the second two are the same as each other. But, they all sound different, and get different results. You have to test your market to see which gets the best results.

By far, the most-used method of giving extra is the sale. *Sale* is a magic word in business; but people are suspicious of phony sales. Some companies pretend to be going out of business when they really aren't. They make you think that their stuff is very cheap, because they must get rid of it before they close their doors. This is not fair and there are laws against this type of business practice. Lying to your customers is the fastest way to go out of business.

Sometimes you want to make a limited time offer or give something away for a short time only. These are legitimate ways of giving the customer incentive to buy.

Two Ways to Give Your Customer a Bargain

This week only. Puppets $10.00 each a $5.00 saving! Usually $15.00

This week only. Buy a puppet for $15.00 and get $5.00 off your next purchase.

WHAT IS THE PUBLIC RELATIONS AND ADVERTISING BUSINESS?

As you can see, it takes talent to think up ways to market a business. I bet you're not surprised to learn that you can sell that talent if you have it. It's called being a *public relations agent* or *consultant*. Many people do the job of getting businesses better known. They call the radio and T.V. stations. They write press releases and they handle promotional events.

Other people are in a related business called *advertising*. They create and write the ads, buy the airtime on radio or T.V., or the space in print. Many of them get creative awards for their work.

ISN'T ADVERTISING DIFFICULT?

Advertising is not hard. You may think that it is harder for a kid, but it is not. You can make your posters, business cards, and flyers at home with construction paper and markers. You can also make all those things on your home computer if you have the right software.

There are a few things that are good to put in your brochures. It's good to have a *logo* (a symbol that signifies your business) or a picture of your own face on your brochure or ad. List the three most important benefits of what you are selling. Be sure the ads let your readers know how to find you and what your goods or services cost.

There is an eleven-year-old girl in Pennsylvania named Sami Akbari who is in the business of making flyers for other kids in business. So, helping people to advertise and market their business is a business in itself.

TESTIMONIALS

A *testimonial* is a statement of praise made by a person who has used your product or service. Testimonials show that you have satisfied customers. You can use testimonials in your advertising by putting them in brochures, reading them on radio, or putting them in your newspaper ads.

Things to Do

Call or write to the Direct Marketing Association (1120 Avenue of the Americas, New York, NY 10036; 212-768-7277) in order to get more information about marketing and advertising.

15

Skill 9:
Networking

DEFINITION

Networking is a way to expand a business by helping others. Meet as many people as you can whom you can help. Do favors for them. You might get something in return.

KEEP NAMES OF SUPPLIERS

When you buy a product from a certain company all the time, you should keep the company's business card so that you can call them if you need help with something or if you have a problem with their product. If they do something nice for you, you should do something for them, like giving away some of your services free or a charging a lower price.

WHY HAVE A NETWORK?

The reason to have a network is so that when you do something for somebody else, that person or company will give something to you. They can do a lot of things for you. They can refer business, too. That means that if they know any people who could benefit from your services, they will tell those people about your business. Another thing that they can do for you is give you free services or products.

WHAT CAN YOU DO FOR OTHERS?

You can offer lower prices or free services to people who help you out. You can also refer business to people who help you.

WARNING

When picking out the people you want in your network, be sure that they have products or services you can use. Also, make sure that the people in your network are the kind of people or companies who will do something for you.

16

Skill 10:
Human Relations

Human relations is the way that you interact with other people. Human relations is also about figuring out what a person's habits are and then later accommodating their habits in your business.

KNOW PEOPLE'S NEEDS

When you go into business you need to know what people in your area's needs are. That knowledge can help you choose what business you will go into. If you already have a business, this can help you in a different way: You can change your business to suit your customers' needs. If your business suits the needs of your community, you will have a good business. For example, if there is no pet-sitting service in your community and a lot of people go there on vacation, then you might decide to start a pet-sitting business.

KNOW THE HABITS OF THE PEOPLE AROUND YOU

In business, it is important to know the habits of the people around you. A good example of a business in which you can use this skill is the business in which you go to the library to exchange books for your whole family (see Business 9). If the book that a particular family member wanted is out, what will you do? If you know what kind of books this person likes to read, you can pick out another book for him or her. If you don't know, you probably won't get anything for that person. That might make the person mad.

BE COURTEOUS AND POLITE

When you talk to people in business, you have to be nice to them. You should never be rude, even if a person is giving you a hard time. Always use good manners. When you are dealing people who have complaints about your business, you should always be sensitive to their needs and try to help them as best as you can.

Part 3

Twenty Super Businesses You Can Start Right Now

17

Two Big Businesses for Kids

BUSINESS 1: HEALTHY LEMONADE STAND
The Big Picture

Lemonade? Oh no, not another lemonade stand! Yes, the old standby is back, but it's different! This lemonade stand has a nineties health-conscious spin. It sells only preservative-free, low-sugar lemonade. Only fresh lemons, distilled or filtered water, and a little bit of sugar are used. Serve carob cookies or other healthy treats of your choice. Cookbooks will give you great ideas for all kinds of delicious homemade, good-for-you snacks.

Here's how to start this healthy business:

❑ Buy the supplies you need to make your lemonade and other treats.

❑ Test the amount of each ingredient for the best taste and to create an "original" recipe (good for advertising). Try different amounts of everything. Taste test with your family.

❑ Set up your selling stands at the same location at the same times each week and advertise so people will know you are there. In front of your home or on your porch is OK. Even better is a busy location like a safe shopping area.

Here's a twist for the lemonade! Work with a public organization or charity to share the profits, and get the use of their grounds in return. For example, outside schools on Friday afternoons, outside places of worship after services, and outside libraries after they close on Saturdays are all locations that can work for you.

Once your business is up and running, you can *franchise* it. Give your friends a contract to use your recipe, advertising, and supplies. They can also use your business name, signs, and marketing techniques. In return, they pay you cost for the supplies and a flat fee to go into your lemonade business. Like Burger King and McDonald's, you can become a franchise mogul.

Here's one area where the government protects business. You can trademark your name and copyright your recipes if they are really unique. That way, no one can use them without your permission. All it costs is a few dollars and lots of paperwork. To learn more write:

United States Copyright Office
Library of Congress
101 Independence Avenue S.E.
Washington, DC 20559-6000

$$-$$$$

This business can create a lot of profit if you stick with it. Another way that you can turn lemon yellow into green is by using the franchise idea. That can really help you be known throughout your town. Ask your friends if they would like to have a franchise.

Kid's Capital

The capital you must put up for this job is very high. You will need money to buy your supplies, money to set up your stand, money for advertising and marketing, and money for recipe books. You will also need time to make the lemonade and the other treats to sell, time to scout out areas where you can sell your products, time to make signs to advertise, and in the end, time to get your franchise going.

" Franchising is a great way to make a lot of money in this business. If you can get a lot of franchises, you can have a full-blown business." —Marvin Mogul

Skills

The skills needed for this business are as follows: You will need to know how to get your business started by testing the lemonade and other treats, how to find places to sell your products, how to start a franchise, and how to

Steps to Success
- ❏ Collect all the materials you will need.
- ❏ Make test batches of lemonade and treats, and test them with your family.
- ❏ Scout out places to sell your lemonade and treats.
- ❏ Sell the lemonade and treats.
- ❏ Set up franchises.

keep your business going for a long time. Perhaps the most important skill that is needed is record keeping.

" To be successful in this business, you must be able to keep good records. If you keep good records, you will know if your business is making money or losing money. Record keeping is the key."
—Successful Sam

BUSINESS 2: DESIGNER DOLLARS
The Big Picture

This business is for the artistically inclined. You create sweatshirts and T-shirts with your own designs on them or use stencils. Use cloth paint, glitter, buttons, and anything else you can think of. You should use quality sweats and T-shirts for your garments. If you use better quality materials, you can get a better price when you sell.

Steps to Success

❑ Buy all your supplies.
❑ Produce one to five sample shirts.
❑ See which designs you and your family like best.
❑ Get a table at a flea market or county fair, or sell to stores.
❑ Keep your designs fresh and trendy.

For example, you can use Hanes or Fruit of the Loom. Another idea, instead of making up your own designs, is making *personalized* shirts. That means you can put whatever the customer wants on the shirt, for example, the person's name and a design.

As for where to sell your product, the possibilities are endless. You can go to county fairs, flea markets, and expos. If you want to go into stores with your product, you can do that in many ways. You can sell on *consignment*, which means that you give a store your product to sell, and if people buy it, the store pays you. If nobody buys your product from the store, the store gives it back to you. For more information on consignment, see page 115. You can also sell your products to the store outright. That means that the store can't give back any of your goods. You might want to sell to baby stores or clothing stores.

You can also sell *wholesale*, which means that a person buys a lot of one product and you give them a discount. That would be the way to sell to stores. Another way to sell would be by working with a charity. For example, whenever a person buys a shirt, a percentage of your earnings would go to the charity.

This business requires a *marketable skill*. That means you have a skill that can be sold as part of your goods and services—in this case, textile designing.

That brings me to one of the hardest parts of going into business: pricing. *Pricing* in this business means how much you are going to charge for your shirts. It's up to you; the pricing of this product is very difficult. It depends on many things. One of the major things is the quality of the shirts you use. For example, if you use Fruit of the Loom shirts instead of a no-brand-name shirt, you can charge more. You should take into account all your expenses when pricing. Also, you should always check out the competition's pricing before you price your own goods. You might want to visit Kids "R" Us and department stores to check prices of similar goods. If you stencil in the designs on your shirts, you might want to charge less than the stores. If you do the design freehand, and it's good, you can charge more. To give you an idea of an appropriate price, I checked with a girl who does this, and she charges $12 for a sweatshirt and $8 for a T-shirt. The sizes are for children three to six years old. The designs are stenciled, and she personalizes the shirts.

$$$-$$$$

This business can be very profitable. If you know where to go to sell your product, and if you are a good salesperson, you will make a lot of money. Also, if your shirts look nice, you will sell a lot of them.

Kid's Capital

The capital needed for this business is very high. You will need a lot of money to buy your supplies. (The Rag

Shop, found in many malls, advertises shirts for $6.88 and paints at two for $1.00; Pearl Paint, 308 Canal Street, New York, NY 10013-2572, has a large selection of paints and glitters at discount prices, and will ship. For a catalog, write to them c/o Catalog Department, send $1.00 and your address.) And you will need money to get tables at flea markets. You will also need time to get your supplies, time to make your shirts, and time to go around selling your products to stores.

" *When you buy your supplies to make your shirts, comparison shop. You will probably be able to save some money that way.*" —Penelope Pennypincher

Skills

The skills needed for this business are as follows: You will need to have *supply savvy,* which means that you must be able to find the supplies that you need at the lowest price possible. You will also need to know how to paint or stencil in the designs that go on your shirts. And you will need to know how to to sell your product.

" *To be successful in this business, you must be able to plan well. You must know how long it takes to produce one shirt, when and where the flea markets are, and how much profit you make on each shirt. In this business, planning is the key.*"
                                    —Successful Sam

18

Seven Old Standbys with Moneymaking Twists

These businesses are ones you may already have tried or read about. They are the traditional kids' businesses. But with our new skills, they all have a new moneymaking twist.

BUSINESS 3: RAKING IN THE MONEY
The Big Picture

Leaf raking is a time-honored job for kids. It's easy, it can be fun, and it's also needed in suburbia far and wide. People who may need kids to perform this task for them are: the elderly and those who just don't have enough time. All that has to be done for this business is to ask potential customers if they need raking done. You can do front yards and/or backyards. You can charge different amounts for different-size yards. If you are a city kid, you'll find some brownstone houses have gardens in the back. There might be some trees there that have leaves. You could rake those leaves.

$$-$$$$

The leaf raking job can be very profitable. The profit will depend on how big your customers' lawns are, how often you come to rake, and how much you charge.

Steps to Success
- ☐ Buy rakes and garbage bags.
- ☐ Put up signs around town.
- ☐ Visit all new customers.
- ☐ Rake and bag the leaves.

Kid's Capital

The capital that is needed for this business is mostly time, but some money is needed, too. Money will be needed for advertising and for supplies. The supplies that will be needed are as follows: one or two rakes (rakes may break, so having an extra couldn't hurt), and plastic garbage bags for carrying the leaves. There is one more thing that you may want to buy, but it's optional: a wheelbarrow. You might want to have one to carry all your supplies back and forth from your jobs. Wheelbarrows can be expensive, so only buy one if you need to.

" This is one of my personal-favorite businesses. I like it because it is so easy and can make a profit." —Marvin Mogul

Skills

The skills needed for this business are as follows: marketing, human relations, and negotiating.

" To be successful in this business, you must know your customers very well. When you know your customers, you will better understand their needs." —Successful Sam

BUSINESS 4: LAWN MOWING SERVICE
The Big Picture

The lawn mowing business can be a pleasure to undertake, but there can be a major expense involved: a lawn mower. You probably can't afford to purchase your own lawn mower, so if you have one, you're doing great. If not, you could consider saving up for one or striking a deal with your parents. If they buy a lawn mower, you give them a percentage of your profits. Lawn mowers can also be rented, or the person who's lawn you're mowing may have one.

The actual service you provide is mowing the lawns of the people in your neighborhood. If your mower is state-of-the-art, feature that in your advertising. That will help you drum up more business. You can charge different prices for different-size lawns. Your target customers will be the elderly and those who just don't have enough time.

$-$$$$

This job can make a huge amount of money if you already have a lawn mower and there are a lot of lawns in your neighborhood. If you do not have a lawn mower and have to rent one, don't start the business without factoring in the cost per

Steps to Success
- [ ] Put up ads around your neighborhood.
- [ ] Gather your equipment.
- [ ] Negotiate a contract with each customer.
- [ ] Show up on time to mow the lawns.

hour of renting. You can create income for a friend by renting a mower from him or her, instead of from a company.

Kid's Capital

This business requires different amounts of capital depending on your situation. If you already have a lawn mower, all you need is the time to mow the lawns and a little bit of money to buy gas for the mower once in a while. If you do not have a mower, the capital is much greater. You need to buy or rent a mower, mow the lawns, and buy gas for the mower.

" Make sure that the gas that you buy for the mower is environmentally safe. Strict environmentalists don't approve of power lawn mowing at all. If you are one of those, use a rotary, push-it-yourself mower. That will help you sell to your customers."

—Responsible Rhoda

Skills

The skills needed for this business are: advertising, human relations, and negotiating. A useful additional skill includes telephoning: using the yellow pages to find lawn mower rental companies and to get the best price.

" To be successful in this business, dependability and consistency are the keys. Choose a time to show up and mow for each house regularly."   —Successful Sam

BUSINESS 5: NURSERY DUTY
The Big Picture

Hey, it's a dirty job, but somebody has to do it. Nursery duty is a business in which you offer three different services to your clients. The first service is nursery cleaning; you offer to clean the nurseries of parents with little children. You should use only environmentally safe products because you are a *novelty* (rare in your field) when you use nontoxic products. The second service is selling environmentally safe cleaning products, the same products that you use for cleaning nurseries. Your customers can use those products for the rest of the house. The third service is diaper cleaning. This service is needed by people who have babies who use cloth diapers; you collect the dirty cloth diapers, clean them, make them sterile, and send them back to their owners.

$$-$$$$

This business can be a good moneymaker. Your profit depends on three factors. The first factor is the price that

Steps to Success

- ❏ Place ads around town.
- ❏ Buy cleaning products to be resold.
- ❏ Make a list of each customer's needs.
- ❏ Negotiate a contract with each customer.
- ❏ Report on time to each customer's house for work.

you charge for your services and products. The second factor is the price that you have to pay for the products you resell. The third factor is which services you provide. All three will make money individually, but doing two or three would be better.

Kid's Capital

This business requires a lot of capital. You will need money to place ads and to buy the products you are selling. You will also need time to do the cleaning needed by your clients.

" Make sure that all the products you use are environmentally safe. That might be very important to your customers."

—Responsible Rhoda

Skills

Advertising is one of the most important skills needed to perform this job. Being able to negotiate will be an important asset as well. Also, knowing how to clean would be good!

" To be successful in this business, you must always come on time and do a complete job."   —Successful Sam

BUSINESS 6: ARTHUR'S GOOD GARBAGE
The Big Picture

Arthur's Good Garbage is really compost, which is the stuff that you get when you let leaves and other organic materials get attacked by heat. All those organic things give off nitrogen, a gas that helps plants to grow.

People who like to garden will want to buy your product because it will help them have a good garden. They will buy it at a good price because it is very expensive to buy in the plant shops. When I was younger, this is one of the businesses I was in. I really enjoyed it a lot.

$$$$

Compost is a great way to make money because profits are high and you don't have many costs. You can sell your bags of compost for $10 each. Package them in ten-pound sizes.

Kid's Capital

You will need leaves from your garden, a rake, some banana peels or other organic material (they go into the pile of compost with other organic stuff), and plastic garbage

Steps to Success

❑ Make sure you have enough compost to fill all your orders.

❑ Keep your compost in neat piles.

❑ Keep your prices competitive with those of major companies.

❑ Keep good records of your sales and your advertising costs.

❑ Make nice packages out of your plastic bags.

bags to put your compost in when it's ready to be sold. You will also need a place to store the compost while it is composting.

Skills

The main skills that you need for this project are advertising and marketing. You need to be able to get the word out about your new business.

" To be successful, you must be able to charge good prices, and you must be able to let people know about your business through advertising. This business works best where people garden but rarely make their own compost."
—Successful Sam

" Package compost in small, colorful bags tied with ribbon and sell it as designer garbage for indoor-plant lovers. It could become the next craze."
—Marvin Mogul

BUSINESS 7: PROFITS FROM PLANTS

The Big Picture

Outdoor and indoor plants are very expensive, but if your family is like mine, they love flowers and greenery. There are two ways you can save money on plants and even create a big business. First, don't let your family's plants die; be in charge of watering, pruning, and feeding. Second, learn how to take cuttings from plants, root them, and grow them into large, healthy plants. If you do this well enough at home, you can even start a home-based plant-sale business right in your own front yard.

$$$$

If you know how to market, this can be a big business. Every plant you own is a little manufacturer of new plants you can sell.

Kid's Capital

Time and some money are needed for this business. You need to buy rooting material and pots.

Skills

The most important skill needed for this business is business budgeting. You will need to find and use whole-sale suppliers to keep your costs down and your business cost-effective. To be successful in this business, you will also need to find a good place to sell your plants.

" To be successful in this business, you must be able keep good records of how much you make and how much you spend." —Successful Sam

Steps to Success

❏ Use the library to find books on growing plants from cuttings.
❏ Experiment until you have some inventory.
❏ Market your product to your family first if they are frequent plant buyers.
❏ Market to the public.
❏ Keep excellent business records.

BUSINESS 8: GREAT FORTUNES FROM GARAGE SALES

The Big Picture

There are many ways to do a garage sale. The most efficient is by going through your own house and picking out the things that you don't need anymore, have outgrown, or just don't want. Sell these things in your yard or at a flea market.

To have a garage sale, you don't need to have a garage. I don't know who made up the name, but when you sell old things that you don't need around the house, it's called a *garage sale*. I like to call it a *tag sale*, because tagging what you sell is so important. If you can really interest the customer, you can sell stuff at good prices and get rid of a lot of the junk that you have lying around the house.

$

The garage sale is a good way to get rid of all your stuff. However, when you sell your products, you will receive less than you originally paid for them.

" To be successful in the garage sale field, you must be able to have a good attitude toward your customers. When customers are at your sale, treat them with respect."

—Successful Sam

Steps to Success

❑ Make sure that your prices are clearly marked.
❑ Give a short history of each product on the tag if it's interesting or funny.
❑ Ask your parents if your pricing is fair.
❑ Check the weather report.
❑ Set a date for your sale.
❑ Advertise well in advance of the sale.

Don't Forget This Date

When: June 21, 10:00 am.
Where: 40 Central Street
What: The Best Garage Sale of the Summer
       Toys, books & much more!

Free Lemonade

Kid's Capital

The things that you should sell at a garage sale are things that you already have. Most of those things will be games, toys, and the like. The biggest capital that you risk in a garage sale is your time. Paid advertising is good for garage sales, so you may want to make an advertising budget as well. If you don't sell enough things, however, you might lose money.

Skills

The skill that you need most in a garage sale is marketing: being able to get people to come to your sale. Put up signs, put ads on bulletin boards, and even put ads in the newspaper. Marketing is also selling at the right price and making the display look nice.

BUSINESS 9: BARGAINS IN BOOKS
The Big Picture

This project is for the family that likes to read and buys lots of books, newspapers, and magazines. Here's how to help save money: If you have a lot of books that you have already read, have outgrown, or that are just not fun anymore, you can trade them in for new books at a book-barter store. The books will probably be used, but you will probably find one that you have never read.

You can also compare the cost of subscription buying with the price of purchasing individual newspapers and magazines. And, most important, you can set up a home library delivery service for your family. Take their book orders and go to the library once a week to fulfill them and return the books they have finished.

Steps to Success

- ❏ Gather your family's old or used books.
- ❏ Bring the books to a book exchange and get new books.
- ❏ Take orders from family members for the library.
- ❏ Make sure that you deliver the books to the library on time.

" The library also has CDs, videos, records, and 16 millimeter films available free."
—Marvin Mogul

$-$$$

This project can be a big money saver if you do it a lot. If you go to the library on a schedule and stick with it, you can save a lot.

Kid's Capital

The only capital that you need for this is time. You will need time to go back and forth to the library, to take orders for books from your family, and to get books from your house to trade in for new books.

Skills

The most important skill needed is human relations: how you talk to people. You need to talk to people in this project because you need to find out what they want from the library. If you can learn your family's tastes, you can continually supply them with books they want even if they don't give you specifics.

" To be successful in this business, you must be able to be on time with your pickups and deliveries."
—Successful Sam

19

A Nifty Idea

I started this book with a nifty idea: that every parent or family does things that waste money in some way, usually in lots of ways. We kids can offer to help stop the waste provided we get a share in the money we help to save.

There's really no need to throw away clothes you can sell, pay full price for food when there are coupons, or be overcharged on your telephone bill. Still, families do it. Why? Because parental units have no time to save money. They waste money to save time, and then they get into bad habits.

Let's save money for our folks by taking the time they won't take to stop waste in the home!

Since I believe that money is right around the corner if you look for it, I started to look at home.

Ever since I wrote *The Totally Awesome Money Book For Kids (and Their Parents)*, I have been on TV talking about money. I am always asked, "How much do you get for an allowance?" The fact is, I don't get an allowance. Ever since I was five, I have been taking and saving the change that my father leaves on the dresser every night. He knows about it; it's not illegal or anything. It's just that he doesn't value that money because it's small change.

Parental Alert: The Annoyance Factor

These businesses are designed to make money by stopping waste in the home. A lot of the stuff you need to do to stop waste requires cooperation from your parental units or a change of habits or both. You can get pretty annoying if you keep nagging your parents about being wasteful. Think about how you feel when they nag you about things.

To prevent annoyance, make sure your folks understand what you are trying to do, and have a signed contract that lists their duties as well as yours. You'll find one on page 67 in Chapter 13 on making contracts. You won't make money without your parents' approval, so keep them as partners in all you do.

BUSINESS 10: COOKING FOR CASH
The Big Picture

A big part of every family's budget is food. So cooking instead of eating out, and growing your own vegetables instead of buying them are ways to save money. But they don't save time. A good way to save money is to find out your family's eating habits. Do your parents eat lunch out when they go to work, or do they bring a bag lunch? How many times a week does your family eat dinner at home?

If your family eats dinner out most nights, you might want to ask your parents if you can eat in more. If your family eats in a lot, try growing your own fruits and vegetables.

After you have convinced your parents to eat in more often, you can take the next step in saving money with food. Instead of buying one package of rice every time your family goes shopping, you can buy the rice *in bulk*, which means that you buy a lot of one product at the same time. For example, buying a ten-pound bag of rice at four dollars is cheaper than buying 10 boxes of rice at 60 cents a pound.

$$$$

This project can be a big moneymaker for you as a consultant if you stick to it.

Kid's Capital

The capital needed here is time. You have to give your time to go shopping with your family, to convince your parents to buy in bulk, and to convince them to eat at home more.

Steps to Success

❑ Find out whether your family eats in or out the most.

❑ Convince your parents to eat in more often.

❑ Try to grow your own fruits and vegetables.

❑ Try to go shopping with your family and buy products in bulk.

❑ Keep good records so that your family will see that they are saving money.

❑ For more resources, send a self-addressed stamped envelope to: Co-op Directory Services 919 21st Avenue South Minneapolis, MN 55404.

Skills

The main skill you will need here is record keeping. If you keep good records of how much you saved by eating in, growing your own fruits and vegetables, and buying in bulk, your parents will keep doing it.

" To be successful in this project, you must be able to keep records, convince your parents, and most important, you must make sure that your family is happy." —Successful Sam

"Stop restaurant madness," Arthur says.

Many times when I go out to dinner with my family, I get the children's menu. I don't like to get it because it makes me think that people think I'm a baby, but I'm not. My parents like it when I get it because they sometimes like the things on the kids' menu. So I order what I want, and they order whatever they want from the kids' menu. This saves them money. They can get what they want cheaper because things are usually cheaper on the kids' menu.

BUSINESS 11: EXTRA CAPITAL FROM COUPONING
The Big Picture

Coupons are a way of giving shoppers a bargain so they will buy a product. The coupons are given by the makers (manufacturers) of the products. Coupons give you money off the price at the cash register, let you buy two for the price of one, or send you back a gift or money in the mail (a *rebate*).

Good shoppers use coupons for the things they want in the first place, not to buy stuff they don't need just because

Steps to Success

❑ Make a filing system based on the foods your family buys the most.
❑ Clip coupons wherever you see them, and place them in order, by food.
❑ Within each food category, file by date, with the expiring coupons up first.
❑ Make a weekly list for the shopper in the family.
❑ Keep track of what you save.

they get money off. But it takes time to find, cut out, and organize coupons. That's why lots of families don't use coupons. That's where you come in as a couponer for profit.

$$

Couponing is very labor intensive, but there is a lot of money to be saved.

Kid's Capital

What you need here is time! time! time! And a little money for magazines and newspapers if your family doesn't already get them. That's where you may find the coupons.

Shopping List

Item	Coupon File	Amount Saved	Brand
Juice	File J (uice).	20	Tropicana
Spaghetti Sauce	File S(auce)	2 for 1	Ragu
Cereal	no coupons	‿‿‿	‿‿‿
milk	File D(airy)	Free cream with gallon of milk	grocery

Skills

The main skill here is organization (record keeping and filing). A coupon filing system showing the dates of expiration and a checklist for the shopper are essential for this project.

Also keep notes on when your coupons expire.

Expiration Date Alert

Orange juice: two-for-one, expires March 3

Garbage bags: 25 cents off, expires April 6

Spaghetti sauce: 30 cents off, today is the last day

"You may have to spend a lot of time on this project, but it will be well worth it come mealtime."
—Responsible Rhoda

Special Note from Arthur

When I researched for this book, I found loads of materials on couponing. There are even couponing clubs and newsletters. If you and your family start to save good money on coupons, look at the bibliography of this book to see how to make it a real family hobby.

BUSINESS 12: RICHES THROUGH REFUNDING
The Big Picture

A *refund* or *rebate* is money you get back when you buy something. The folks who send you the money are usually the manufacturers (the ones who make what you bought). Why do they do it? Sometimes to get you to buy a new product; sometimes to find out who their customers are.

To get your refund, you must fill out a form and also send back a *proof of purchase,* something to show that you really bought the product, for example, the barcode from a carton of toothpaste or a cap from a bottle. The manufacturer will let you know what you need to send in through ads in the paper, signs in the grocery or drugstore, or coupons in the mail.

Steps to Success

❏ Make three files: a bag for bottles, a paper file for receipts, and a box for odd-shaped stuff.

❏ Help the family shopper unpack, and go with him or her to the store as often as you can.

❏ Save labels, proof-of-purchase seals, and Universal Product Code seals. (Fill and soak bottles with hot water to get the labels off.)

❏ Make a list of the weight, size, and manufacturer of the product.

❏ Keep a lookout for refund forms in packages, in stores, and in newspapers.

❏ Ask for more mail! Write to Donnelly Marketing, 1235 North Avenue, Nevada, AZ 50201, and Direct Marketing Association, 6 East 43rd Street, New York, NY 10017.

❏ Ask your family shopper to keep all cash register receipts. You may need them, too.

❏ Keep a list of refund offers and the dates they expire. Give your family shopper a copy of the list of offers and dates.

" To be a success in the refunding trade, you must keep good records of your proofs of purchase and your refund offers."

—Successful Sam

$$

Refunding can make you hundreds of dollars in a year. Average refunds are $1 or $2 per item and can amount to $20 at a time if you purchase a lot of a product.

" You can save even when you spend."
—Steven Spender

Kid's Capital

You'll need a stamp and an envelope for each refund and the time to look through the newspapers and coupon sources for information on refunds.

Skills

The main skills you will need are filing and organization. The big money in refunds comes from buying only what you use anyway, not buying a product just for the refund. So it's best to save proofs of purchase in a well-organized file and use them when you can get a refund.

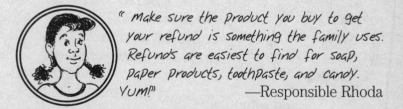

" Make sure the product you buy to get your refund is something the family uses. Refunds are easiest to find for soap, paper products, toothpaste, and candy. YUM!"
—Responsible Rhoda

BUSINESS 13: PACKAGES OF PROFIT—RECYCLING CANS, GLASS, AND PAPER
The Big Picture

Those people interested in preserving our environment do many things to help, like recycling containers, aluminum, and anything else they can find. Did you know that recycling centers will pay you to receive certain types of packaging?

The best moneymakers are:

- ❏ Aluminum, including cans, pie plates, aluminum siding, and window frames
- ❏ Green and clear glass from jars, bottles, and drinking glasses
- ❏ Newspapers, clean and wrapped in bundles of a pound or two in weight

$$

This can be pure profit if your family uses lots of these materials and you're also a good hunter. However, you will never get as much as you or your parents actually paid for the recyclable goods.

Kid's Capital

Very little is needed here except time and storage space. This is a good moneymaker for kids with garages, sheds, or covered patios. Once a month, you'll need transportation to the recycling center. Get help from a grown-up.

" You could use a partner. Does anyone in your family own a truck? If yes, bring them into the business. They will be able to bring you to the recycling plant."
—Marvin Mogul

Skills

The most important skill you will need is networking. The real money is made here by putting out the word that you will accept clean packaging on consignment from friends and neighbors.

" I like the idea of making money and helping our planet at the same time."
—Responsible Rhoda

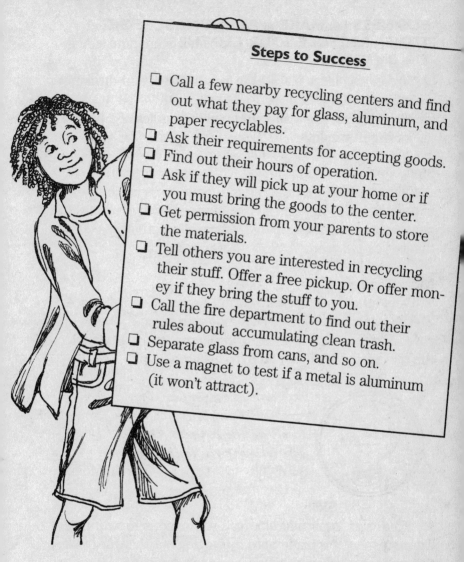

Steps to Success

❏ Call a few nearby recycling centers and find out what they pay for glass, aluminum, and paper recyclables.

❏ Ask their requirements for accepting goods.

❏ Find out their hours of operation.

❏ Ask if they will pick up at your home or if you must bring the goods to the center.

❏ Get permission from your parents to store the materials.

❏ Tell others you are interested in recycling their stuff. Offer a free pickup. Or offer money if they bring the stuff to you.

❏ Call the fire department to find out their rules about accumulating clean trash.

❏ Separate glass from cans, and so on.

❏ Use a magnet to test if a metal is aluminum (it won't attract).

" To be successful in this business, you must be able to keep yourself on schedule with the pickups and drop-offs of your recyclable goods. Make a deal with your parents or your older brother or sister to help you make deliveries. Give them a cut of the profits." —Successful Sam

BUSINESS 14: MAKE A FASHIONABLE FOR-TUNE—RECYCLE YOUR CLOTHES

The Big Picture

A fashionable trend today is to buy used (sometimes called *slightly hurt* or *gently worn*) clothes from resale shops. Kids' clothes sell especially well. We grow so fast, and sometimes it doesn't pay to buy new clothes for us. Even purses, shoes, and hats are in demand. Brand-new items gotten as gifts or bought in the wrong size can be sold for almost full price.

Steps to Success

- ❑ Look in the phone directory under "Used Clothing," "Thrift Shops," "Recycled Clothes," "Resale Shops," and "Children's Clothing."
- ❑ Call the shop and ask: What condition must items be in? What percentage of the sale price do I get? How long do you keep items if they are not sold? Do you return items to me? What if I change my mind and want an item back? Are you part of a charity?
- ❑ Make a list of all the items you want to resell. Ask your family to add to the list.
- ❑ Get your parents' approval for everything on the list.
- ❑ Deliver the bundle to the shop of your choice, and get them to sign the list so you both agree on what's yours.
- ❑ Get your consignment number and keep a record of it.
- ❑ If you haven't done well in a month, try a new place. Or if you have a lot of stuff, test two places at a time.

Resale shops accept your clothes *on consignment.* That means you leave your stuff there, and they assign you a number and tag your clothes with that number. If someone buys your item, they keep a running record of your account and send you a check every month or so, depending on the shop's policy.

$

You receive one-third to one-half of the sale price of the clothes left on consignment. This business is rated low profit only because you will always receive less than your folks originally paid for your clothes, but, of course, you would get nothing if the clothes were thrown out or left to grow old in your drawer.

Kid's Capital

You'll need the clothes themselves, a few phone calls, and the time or money to clean the garments before you bring them into the shop.

"Find out if the shop accepts used toys and books. Most do. There's lots of extra money in used games and puzzles, so try not to lose the pieces to games when you play with them."

—Marvin Mogul

"Collect the stuff that sells best, like baby clothes and baby toys. Ask your aunts, uncles, cousins, and other relatives if they have any extras. Offer them 10 percent of the profits." —Successful Sam

Skills

The key to making money here is record keeping. You must know what you gave in, what was sold, and for how much. Eventually, you can test several stores to decide which are the moneymaking winners, so you'll need your records.

"Instead of reselling, donate the items to charity and help your folks get a tax deduction. That will save them money." —Charitable Charlie

How to Set Up a Home Waste Management Consulting Business

CALL YOURSELF A CONSULTANT

Waste management is a special kind of business, and it takes a special kind of entrepreneur called a *consultant*. The word *consultant* comes from the word *console* and it means to give advice. So you, as a home waste management consultant, must give advice on saving money by cutting down waste in your home. All entrepreneurs, no matter what business they are in, make their money selling something valuable to someone who needs it. Shop owners sell stuff; lawyers sell legal services; gardeners sell their know-how in making things grow.

As a home waste management consultant, you are selling something, too: your good ideas on how to cut down costs or to make money by stopping waste.

Here's what your business card might look like:

```
Jeffrey Jones, W.M.C.
Waste Management Consultant


(817) 555-1208    15 Maplewood Lane
                  Fort Worth, TX 55523
```

GET YOUR VALUABLE IDEAS ON PAPER

Everybody has good ideas, but not everybody can sell them. To get money for your ideas, you have to put them down on paper so people can read them, understand them, and appreciate them. If they can't do all three, you won't get paid.

There is a quick way that consultants do this that doesn't take a writing genius and is lots of fun. It's called an *audit and report*. Because we are home waste management consultants, we will call it the *waste management audit and report*.

An audit is just a look around to see if anything is wrong or if things are OK. The dictionary defines audit as "a regular examination and adjustment." With a written audit, your customer will understand the problem.

For example, your audit might check for leaks that waste water or how tight doors and windows are to see if they waste home heating fuel. Here's an example of an audit for water waste:

WATER WASTE AUDIT FOR JONES FAMILY

Address	15 Maplewood Lane Fort Worth, Texas
Number of faucets and locations	• Sink – 1st floor bathroom • Kitchen sink – 1st floor • Mom & Dad's bath – shower, tub & sink – 2nd floor • Kids' bath – shower and sink - 2nd floor
Leaks	• 1st floor bath – sink • Mom and Dad's bath – 2nd floor tub
Hidden Leaks	• Yes
Toilets	• 3 (one in each bath)
Water-saving devices	• Shower head savers yes no √ • Weights in toilet yes no √ •Turn-off-water signs yes √ no

Just knowing what is wrong is not enough to make you a consultant. You also must know how to solve the problem. You put your ideas in a report that tells your customer how to fix what's wrong, how much it will cost to fix, and who can fix it for them.

With a report, your customer will appreciate what they need to do and how you are helping them. Here's what a report looks like:

REPORT

There are 2 leaks I can see in the first-floor bathroom and second-floor tub. Also, there are no water-saving shower heads or weights in the toilet tank.

RECOMMENDATION

1. Fix two faucets	Cost: $30.00	Sam the plumber 673-2000
2. Replace two shower heads	Cost: $34.00	Linba's Hardware 736 Main Street Open 9–5 til 9 on Thurs
3. Put plastic jar filled with rocks in each tank	Cost: zero	I will do it.

Estimated Savings: $30.00 per month
Average water bill in the past six months: $150.00

As a consultant, you can do just the audit and report, or you can also be the one who fixes the problem. It depends on you and on what the problem is.

For example, let's say you find out that the family flushes the toilet lots of times a day and that putting a plastic jar filled with rocks in the tank can save 2 gallons of water with every flush. Well, that's an easy thing you can do yourself. But let's say you find out that the faucet leaks and needs a new washer. Maybe you can fix it; maybe you need a plumber. In your report, you would include the name of the plumber and the estimated cost.

Which brings me to the next part of the consulting business: getting paid.

WAYS THAT CONSULTANTS GET PAID

As a consultant, you can be paid in four different ways, depending on how you want to run your business.

1. **By the Hour:** You have to put a price on your time, just the way you do if you are baby-sitting. This is called an *hourly rate*. Let's say you want $2.00 an hour. For a baby-sitter, it's easy because the parents just tell you how many hours they want, and you multiply the hours by $2.00 and get paid.

5 hours of baby-sitting at $2.00 an hour = 5 X $2.00 =$10.00

A consultant does the same thing except that he or she sets the amount of time spent. You have to know how long it will take to do the waste management audit and report. You won't really know how much time it will take until you have done a lot of them, so I don't recommend this way of getting paid for a beginner. Most beginners charge too little because they think things will go faster than they do.

2. **By the Audit:** Give one price that you think is fair for the type of work involved. This is called a *fee*. It's the way you might charge to shovel snow or mow a lawn; you look at the size of the yard, you know what others are charging, and you give a price.

Again, beginning consultants can't do this because they don't have enough experience to get to the right price. Adults belong to clubs called *trade associations* where they learn from each other.

" If you want to charge by the hour or by the job, ask others in your business what they charge."

—Marvin Mogul

3. By Getting Part of the Money Your Customer Saves or Gets Because of Your Waste Management Audit Report. Bingo! This is the one for us. Let's say you do the water audit, and it saves the family $30.00. You get part of that savings. Let's say you do an old clothes audit and then sell the clothes to a resale shop; you get part of the money you make. Sometimes this is called a *cut*. That's really slang, but it's used all the time. The right word is *percentage*. In this way, you don't need to set a price on your time or the job.

Even more important, it's easy to get hired because the customer doesn't pay you anything unless you get results for them, save or make them money.

4. Don't Forget to Charge for Extra Work: In addition to the fee, hourly rate, or cut you get for the audit and report, you must charge money for any extra work you do to solve the problem, like plumbing, fixing a window, or growing food.

If you charge a fee or an hourly rate, you just set a separate price for added work and put it on the bill. A bill is called an *invoice*. Here's what a consultant's invoice looks like:

INVOICE

From: Penelope Pennypincher
To: The Pennypincher Family   Date: July 14,1995

Work performed: Waste Management Audit and Report
Time Spent: Three hours, July 10, 1995

Hourly rate: $2.50

Balance due: $7.50

Fixing faucet: $10.00

Total balance due: $17.50

If you get paid with a cut of savings or earnings, you get paid for doing these extras by taking a bigger cut. The more you do over and above the audit and report, the bigger your cut must be. For example:

INVOICE

From: Penelope Pennypincher   Date: July 14,1995
To: The Pennypincher Family

Work performed: Waste Management Audit and Report
Amount Saved from July 10 to August 10: $30.00

Percent due: 50% = $15.00

Balance due: $15.00

Fixing faucet: $10.00

Total balance due: $25.00

Note that you made more money with a percentage. But (1) you have to be sure the family actually saves money or you get nothing, and (2) you have to wait to get paid until you know how much they saved.

Know What It Costs to Start the Business and to Keep It Going

Every business needs time or money or both to get started and to keep going. This is called *capital.* For grown-ups, capital is almost always money. For us, capital is mostly our time. But some of the jobs in this book require money, too, especially for advertising and supplies.

Some take low amounts of capital; some take a lot. This is called *low or high start-up costs.* Some jobs take large amounts of your time. They are called *labor intensive.* Some take little time or capital. They are called *cost-effective.* Fill in this chart for some of the jobs in this book:

Job	Capital: high/low	Type of Capital: time/money	Amount of Labor high/low
1.			
2.			
3.			
4.			
5.			
6.			
7.			
8.			
9.			
10.			
11.			
12.			

MAKE A DEAL WITH YOUR CUSTOMER TO DO THE WORK

Before you start work as a consultant, you must have a deal with your customer. The deal is an agreement between you about:

❏ What the work is.
❏ When the work will be finished.
❏ How much you will be paid.
❏ When you will be paid.
❏ What happens if you don't do the job.

These deals can also include other things, depending on the work involved.

After you make the deal, you must put it in writing. This is called a *contract.* You'll find an example on page 67.

To make the deal fair for everyone, you need to be a good negotiator. Negotiating is an important business skill that you learned about in Chapter 12.

All these things are important to running a successful business. On the following pages, you will learn about the many consulting jobs and businesses in which you will have to use some, if not all, of the things that you have just learned. If you need to look back at what you have just learned, don't be afraid! No one will think the less of you!

MAKING MONEY BY BECOMING A WASTE DETECTIVE

This chapter shows you five different ways that you can find and get rid of waste in the home; each will save your family money. Here's where the notebook comes in handy.

Just read the list of the types of waste in the table of contents. Take a family stop-waste survey. Ask your parental units and older siblings where they think the family can save the most money.

Spark their imagination by reviewing the waste saving business. It will give them ideas of which jobs and activities will do them the most good, i.e., telephone surveys, water surveys, electricity and utility surveys.

BUSINESS 15: TREASURE HUNTING WITH A TELEPHONE AUDIT

The Big Picture

Not too long ago, there wasn't much you could do to save money on telephone calls except talk less. Today, there's lots of competition, and many telephone companies are out to win your business.

To act as a telephone consultant, you can compare the costs of different companies, go over your family's monthly bill to make sure there are no mistakes, and break down the bill by type of call to see if money can be saved by using letters, postcards, or faxes.

$$$

They call my mom "the Touch-Tone Kid." So, at least in my family, we can save a lot with a telephone audit. Your family might be the same, or it might be different.

Kid's Capital

After you have done a telephone audit once, it will only take minutes a month.

Steps to Success

❑ Learn to read the phone bill.

❑ Look at the charges you pay for renting your phones.

❑ Discuss buying phones with your folks.

❑ Call various telephone companies to get their long-distance charges. Each company has many different plans.

❑ Look at the bills to see which plan fits the way your family makes calls.

❑ Give your family a report to see if they want to change long-distance phone companies.

❑ Get an 800-number telephone directory; 800-number calls are free and can save you money.

❑ Give everyone a list of the numbers they use most. This way they won't be tempted to use Directory Assistance to find the numbers. Every time they do, it costs about 30 cents.

❑ Check the bill every month for adding mistakes, calls the family didn't make, and things that just look wrong, like a very long call or one to a place where you have no relatives or friends.

❑ Share your findings with your family. If they confirm a mistake, you can take care of it.

"These phone audits can save you a lot of money, and your parents might let you talk on the phone more."
—Successful Sam

Skills

The most important skill you will need is complaining. You have to get things straightened out if the bill is wrong.

```
Account Number                    Statement Date              Page   1 of 5
                                    Apr  8, 1995

                For Billing Questions 24 Hours a Day - 7 Days a Week
        Call 1-800-222-0300 (Voice) or 1-800-833-3232 (Text Telephone)
```

AT&T   Your AT&T True USA℠ Savings this month:
                                        $9.54

Summary of AT&T Activity

Previous Charges

Amount of Last Bill	131.35
Payments (See Detail Page 5)	131.35℄
	$.00

Current Charges

Bill Section	Page	Calls	Minutes	Amount
Total Charges for True USA℠ Savings	2-4	41	215	38.15
Direct Dial Calls	4	11		8.85
Card Calls	5	1		1.55
Taxes and Surcharges	5			4.10
				$52.65

Total Summary of AT&T Activity		53	215	$52.65
Payment Due by May 7, 1995			

TEAR HERE

AT&T

Account Number	Statement Date	Payment Due Date	New Balance	Enter Amount Enclosed
	Apr 8 1995	May 7 1995	$52.65	$.

Please return this portion with your payment.
Make check payable to AT&T.
Please include account number on payment.

Make changes to name, address, and telephone number:
Name
Address
City   State   Zip
Home Telephone   Business Telephone

000293-004915 1 ZP .267
**C007
0517016126401-113 SC28

AT&T
P.O. BOX 8211
FOX VALLEY   IL
60572-8211

0517016126401113280000000052650000000526500000052659

The following companies will send you information on their costs; your report should compare them:

Allnet: 1-800-783-2020
AT&T: 1-800-222-0300
Metromedia: 1-800-275-2273
MCI: 1-800-444-3333
Sprint: 1-800-877-4000

BUSINESS 16: EARN HONORS FOR HOME OFFICE AUDITS

The Big Picture

Your parents have a home office, though they may not think of it that way. Every family has a place where they write their checks, pile up mail, and do other work. Usually, it's the kitchen table. Some of your parents may have a separate room, a computer, or even a real secretary who comes to the house.

Where's the money in this? Just like utilities and shop-

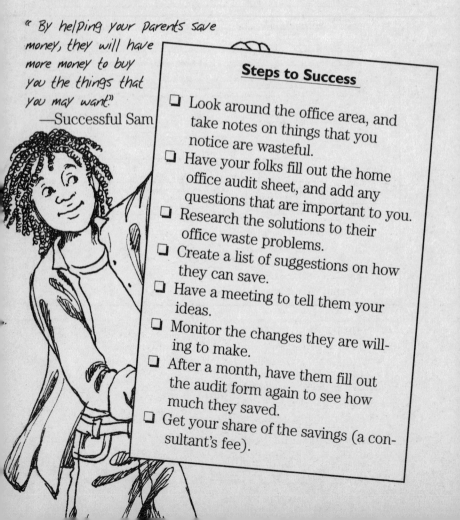

" By helping your parents save money, they will have more money to buy you the things that you may want."
—Successful Sam

Steps to Success

❏ Look around the office area, and take notes on things that you notice are wasteful.

❏ Have your folks fill out the home office audit sheet, and add any questions that are important to you.

❏ Research the solutions to their office waste problems.

❏ Create a list of suggestions on how they can save.

❏ Have a meeting to tell them your ideas.

❏ Monitor the changes they are willing to make.

❏ After a month, have them fill out the audit form again to see how much they saved.

❏ Get your share of the savings (a consultant's fee).

ping, there's a lot of waste that goes along with a home office. Depending on how much work your parents do at home, you may be able to make good money as a home waste management consultant. Do a home office audit, and get paid a part of the amount you help them save.

The money you earn from this work depends on how good you are at spotting waste, finding solutions, and making them work. It also depends on how much work your parents actually do at home.

Kid's Capital

Time is the only capital you need. But, remember that consultants spend only their time, which is very valuable capital.

Skills

Research is the main skill you will need. As a consultant, you need to find out better ways of doing things, better places to buy things, and things that are done but that don't have to be done at all. All this takes knowing how to find solutions for problems. For example, if your mom or dad spends a lot of money on stamps, maybe bulk mail is the solution. You'll have to visit the post office to find out all the ways that mail can be sent cheaper than first class—that's research.

Here's a sample home office audit:

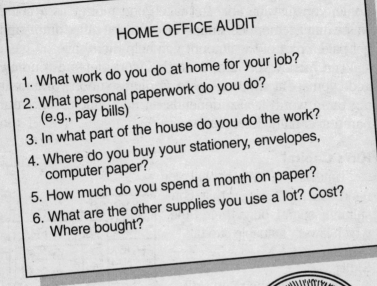

HOME OFFICE AUDIT

1. What work do you do at home for your job?

2. What personal paperwork do you do?
   (e.g., pay bills)

3. In what part of the house do you do the work?

4. Where do you buy your stationery, envelopes,
   computer paper?

5. How much do you spend a month on paper?

6. What are the other supplies you use a lot? Cost?
   Where bought?

*" Don't forget to do separate
telephone and utility audits."*
—Marvin Mogul

JUST A FEW SAVING HINTS FOR THE HOME OFFICE

❏ Use both sides of computer paper if you are printing drafts.

❏ Sell used paper to a recycler (see Business 13).

❏ Buy checks through the mail instead of from the bank. Call Checks In The Mail, 1-800-733-4443, and Currents, Inc., 1-800-426-0822. The cost is about $5.00 for 200 checks instead of the $12.00 banks charge. At a fee of 50 percent of the savings, you earn $3.50 every time your folks write 200 checks.

❏ Buy office furniture at thrift shops. Make pen and pencil holders from painted jars.

BUSINESS 17: WATER WORKS
The Big Picture

The water works project is a fun way to help save the environment and save some money at the same time. This is how it works: Water costs money; and when you have leaks in your water system, it can be costly to your family and to the environment. To help save the environment and save money, go around your house and look for leaks. Some secret hiding places are: in faucets, behind the walls, and even sometimes in toilets. Did you know that 20 percent of the toilets in people's homes are leaking right now?

Here's a good way to check for leaks. Ask your parents or any adult in your house to show you how to read the water meter. When the whole family goes out, check the meter, and write down the number. Make sure nobody is in the house. When you come back, check the meter again. If the number is different from what it was when you left, you probably have a leak.

Did you know that the freshest drinking water in your house is in the toilet bowl (before you use it)? It's true. Be especially careful to look for leaks in the toilet bowl. When flushed, a toilet bowl can use over 7 gallons of water. There are lots of ways to save some of that water.

To save water when flushing the toilet, put a 1– or 2–gallon bottle (say, an empty plastic one from dishwashing fluid) in the back of the tank, with rocks in the bottom of it to keep it stationary. You will save 1 to 2 gallons of water every time you flush just by doing that.

$$

You can save a lot of money when you find leaks. You also have to take care of them, and make sure that they get fixed.

Kid's Capital

This is a cost-efficient business. That means that you make a good profit with very low costs or very little time put into the business.

Skills

Record keeping is the main skill you need because you have to show your parents that you are saving them money.

Steps to Success

- ❏ Make sure you know how to read the water meter.
- ❏ Check around the house for any type of leak.
- ❏ Tell your parents about the leaks.
- ❏ Get the leaks fixed.

"To be successful in this business, you must be able to talk to your parents to find out how to read the water meter."

—Successful Sam

You also need record keeping because you need to remember where your leaks are so that you can get them fixed.

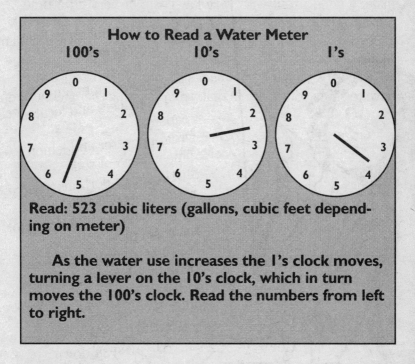

How to Read a Water Meter

Read: 523 cubic liters (gallons, cubic feet depending on meter)

As the water use increases the 1's clock moves, turning a lever on the 10's clock, which in turn moves the 100's clock. Read the numbers from left to right.

BUSINESS 18: REVENUES FROM RESTAURANT SAVINGS
The Big Picture

If your family eats out a lot, there's a fortune to be saved with a restaurant audit.

You'll have to track the number of times they eat out, where they eat, and how much they spend for a whole month. Then you can show them how to cut the cost without cutting the fun. And you get a cut of the savings.

$-$$$$

The money you make will vary with how often your family eats out and how much they spend.

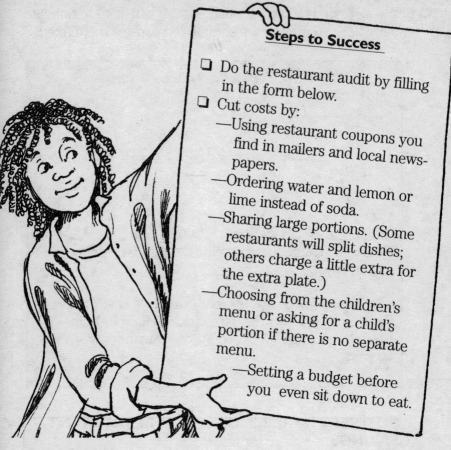

Steps to Success

- ❑ Do the restaurant audit by filling in the form below.
- ❑ Cut costs by:
  —Using restaurant coupons you find in mailers and local newspapers.
  —Ordering water and lemon or lime instead of soda.
  —Sharing large portions. (Some restaurants will split dishes; others charge a little extra for the extra plate.)
  —Choosing from the children's menu or asking for a child's portion if there is no separate menu.
  —Setting a budget before you even sit down to eat.

Kid's Capital

This business will require very little in time and no dollar cost at all.

Skills:

The skills needed are record keeping and human relations. You'll have to keep receipts and even menus to make the most effective money-saving plans. Food is a touchy subject; you'll have to make sure that your family is happy at meals and doesn't feel as though they are depriving themselves by not eating out as much.

" To be successful in this business, you must keep your family happy while you're saving money. Always make sure that your family gets what they want to eat.

—Successful Sam

Restaurant Audit

Times a week we eat out: __4__

Where we eat out: _Chinese takeout, Zanelli's Italian, Shrimp_
House

How much we spend on average for meal:
_$30.00–$45.00_

Food _$29.00_

Drinks _$6.00_

Dessert _-0-_

Tip _$5.25_

Tax _$2.50_

TOTAL _$42.75 x 4= $171.00 a week!_

Restaurant Report

We can save $69.00 a week if we eat out one time a week instead of 4.

Dinner with drinks at home = $20.00

$20.00 x 3 = $60.00
      + $42.00 for one meal out
         $102.00 instead of $171.00

TOTAL SAVINGS: $69.00

BUSINESS 19: HEALTHY PROFITS FROM HEAT AUDITS
The Big Picture

They say that more heat is lost off the top of your head than from any other part of the body. So if you wear a hat, you keep 80 percent of the warmth in your body. I learned that a house is like that, too. If you do just a few things, you can save a big part of the fuel bill.

You don't have to know anything about heating or science to save lots of money in this business, but it helps. You will learn a lot about energy as you go along. The best part is that your utility company will do an energy audit for you and teach you ways that you can save energy and money.

$$$$

If your family owns their own house, this is probably the biggest moneysaver in the book.

Kid's Capital

You don't need anything but your time. But a few of your suggestions will take big money if your parents want to follow them. So make sure your audit compares the costs with the savings.

Skills

You'll need lots of skills for this business, especially telephoning, organization (record keeping and filing), and human relations.

" *Cutting waste on your heating bill will save your parents a lot of money. Also, you will feel more comfortable in the house.*"
                                              —Successful Sam

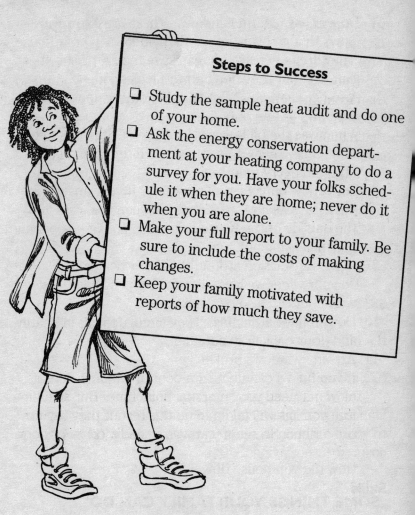

Steps to Success

☐ Study the sample heat audit and do one of your home.

☐ Ask the energy conservation department at your heating company to do a survey for you. Have your folks schedule it when they are home; never do it when you are alone.

☐ Make your full report to your family. Be sure to include the costs of making changes.

☐ Keep your family motivated with reports of how much they save.

Heat Audit

1. What kind of energy heats your house: oil, gas, solar, or electric?
2. What company supplies the fuel (name, address, and telephone number)?
3. What was the average monthly fuel bill last year?

4. Do you have storm windows? These are extra windows that go over the regular windows in your house. They are expensive but can save fuel. A plastic sheet can, too, but they don't always look good.
5. Are there air leaks? Put your hand near doors and windows to find out.
6. When was the oil burner last cleaned? It needs to be done three times a year, and the filter should be changed every month.
7. Does snow on your roof melt fast? If your answer is yes, the insulation (the stuff between the walls and the outside of the house or roof) is not very good, and heat is leaking out.
8. Is there insulation around the water heater?
9. Do your windows have drapes? Drapes keep things warm but can also be expensive.
10. Do you have attic fans? They circulate heat in winter and draw cool air in summer.
11. Are any windows broken?
12. If you hold a candle near a door or window, does it blow out? Ask your parental units for permission before you light a candle to do this test. If they say no, use a ribbon to see if it waves near a window or door.

How did you house do?

SOME THINGS YOUR FAMILY CAN DO
Free:
❏ Lower the thermostat.
❏ Wear a sweater.
❏ Close doors and windows.

For small amounts of money:
❏ Clean the furnace and change the filters.
❏ Use weather stripping.
❏ Fix broken windows.

For a lot of money:
- ❏ Put up drapes.
- ❏ Install a new furnace.
- ❏ Install an attic fan.

You will need to learn to read an electric meter. It has five numbered dials. The pointers on three of the dials turn clockwise, so read from left to right. The pointer always registers the number it has just passed. So if the pointer is between 3 and 4, read the number as 3. Next month read the dials again. That will tell you how many kilowatt-hours were used.

Gas meters are read the same way except there are four dials, two that move clockwise and two that move counterclockwise.

BUSINESS 20: LIGHT UP YOUR BANK ACCOUNT BY SAVING ELECTRICITY
The Big Picture

Like fuel and water, electricity is expensive. Also, you really can't see it, so it's easy to forget you are spending money every time a light or TV is on.

Just by reading the electric meter, looking at the bill, and doing an audit, you will save money. Better yet, all electric utility companies will do a survey for you and help you save.

$$$$

Most families really waste electricity, so savings can be big.

Kid's Capital

This is even better than heat and water waste management because the things you must do to save electricity are very inexpensive and mostly free. So, the capital you need is just your time.

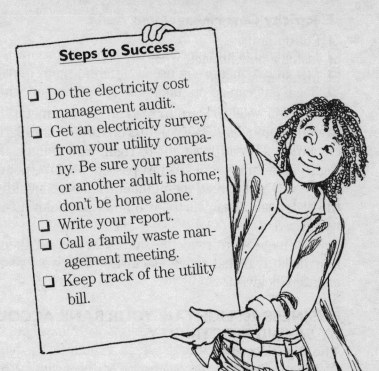

Steps to Success

- ❏ Do the electricity cost management audit.
- ❏ Get an electricity survey from your utility company. Be sure your parents or another adult is home; don't be home alone.
- ❏ Write your report.
- ❏ Call a family waste management meeting.
- ❏ Keep track of the utility bill.

Skills

The most important skill you will need is human relations. Turning on lights and other uses of electricity are habits. You may get yelled at when you first work with your family to save electricity.

"Not only do you save money on this job, but you help save the environment when you use less energy."
—Successful Sam

Electricity Cost Management Audit

❏ List all lights and electrical appliances by room.
❏ List which ones are in use at different times of day.
❏ See if any can go on timers to turn off and on when you need them.
❏ What kind of bulbs are used? *Compact fluorescents* save the most money in electricity and in bulb cost (they are more expensive but they last much longer).
❏ Are the lightbulbs dusted? Dirty ones use more electricity.
❏ Does anyone open the refrigerator door and leave it open? Put up a sign.
❏ Set refrigerator between 38 and 42 degrees. More is too cold and costs money.

Start a Laundromat

When I researched saving electricity, I found out that a clothes dryer costs almost 50 cents an hour to use. I figured that I could save the money and split the savings if I hung up the clothes instead of using the dryer. But, it wasn't worth the time. The savings compared with the time spent was not cost-efficient.

But I still have an idea that if I were good at ironing clothes, I could make money in a cost-efficient way with a home laundromat. I could offer to wash the clothes in a washing machine, hang them in the basement to dry, and then iron them.

I could charge for the work, not just keep part of the savings. At first, this business may not sound good to you, if washing clothes seems like just a chore. But then my mom explained that owning a laundromat is a very good business. Some people who own real ones own whole chains of them. Whichever job you pick, you can learn from others in the business through trade journals. (See the bibliography.)

Extra Ways to Make Extra Money

Since this is a book about not wasting, I didn't want to waste any good ideas that I had for making money. So here is a list of some other things you can do to save money and get a cut, although they probably won't earn enough to build a separate business.

Disposables Audit:

Look for stuff your family throws out that they could save. For example, save aluminum foil to use twice, use cloths instead of paper towels, or step on toilet paper rolls so they won't unravel when you pull them.

Change Scooping:

Don't forget my deal with Dad. If I find change, I keep it.

Start a Buying Service:

If your folks are planning to buy something big, like a refrigerator or car, offer to comparison shop for them. Look through the newspapers and call a number of places listed in the telephone book to get details. Most important, use the classified ads to find what they want secondhand. Give them three leads, and let them follow up.

Junk Art:

If you are a good artist or craftsperson, you can turn junk into sculpture that you can sell at flea markets and garage sales. In New York City, there is a gallery called Galleria Hugo where junk art sells for high prices.

"This is the chapter I've been waiting for."

21

The Big Kahuna

What if you did all the jobs in the book? Every one of them! You would be a complete waste management consultant. Wow! It's possible. Just start with the one that fits you best. Get that business going. Once it's in place, start another business just like it, but in a different area.

This is called *business expansion*. Soon your business might look like this:

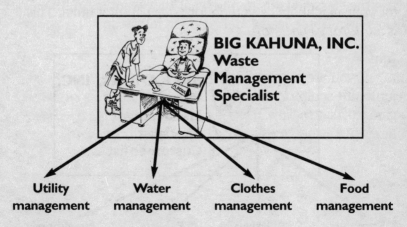

BIG KAHUNA, INC.
Waste
Management
Specialist

Utility management

Water management

Clothes management

Food management

You can expand in a lot of ways. You can keep your waste management business and also go into the resale clothes business I told you about on page 114. These businesses are not related, so really this makes you a *conglomerate*. Some famous conglomerates are RJR Nabisco and Hansen Jacuzzi.

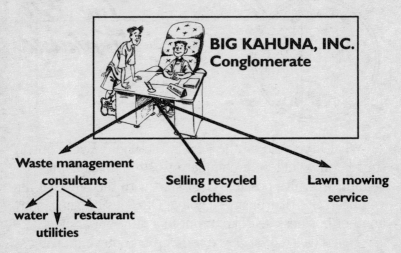

BIG KAHUNA, INC.
Conglomerate

Waste management consultants

water utilities   **restaurant**

Selling recycled clothes

Lawn mowing service

You can take on new customers and do the same thing for your neighbors as you do for your parental units. This is a *lateral expansion*.

BIG KAHUNA, INC.
Waste Management Specialist Customer list

Strangers who become clients   **Relatives**   **Parents**   **Neighbors**

Coca Cola is an example of lateral expansion. They sell Coke in the United States, China, Russia and other countries.

You can make the supplies you need instead of buying them and even sell those supplies. This is a *vertical expansion.*

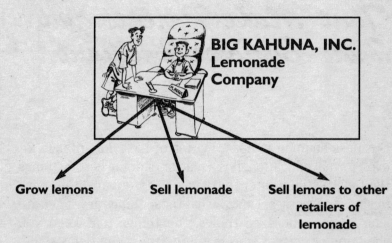

Grow lemons   **Sell lemonade**   **Sell lemons to other retailers of lemonade**

Sunkist, the orange juice people, are an example of vertical expansion.

Epilogue

Ten Super Fun Activities That Make Parents and Kids Business Brilliant

Business acumen is not a matter of luck, inheritance, or even formal education. It is a matter of doing certain things right all the time. After thirty years of studying impressive business successes, I know what those things are. They are simple, commonsense things, the things that keep you shopping at certain stores, visiting the same dentist, and buying at the same flower shop no matter what the competition does. In my own business, the more I do these things, the more I prosper, and vice versa. Here are my top ten best business habits and how to teach/learn them with your kids. You can have fun with these even if your child is not engaged in business at the moment. Just raising consciousness about these business bonanzas is a great step in the right direction.

BE LIKED AND RESPECTED
1. Thank Someone: Who gave you a helping hand recently? Did anyone do a job that was top-notch? It could be the local pizza delivery person who brought the pie while it was still hot. It could be a camp counselor or someone you asked for advice on saving energy. If you try, you

and your child can think of lots of people to thank. Make a list and then thank them in writing. If you know who their boss is, send a duplicate of the thank-you.

Obviously, this exercise can be fun and helps you make and keep friends. But why does it help with business success? Help your child write down all the ways:

- ❏ It wins you new customers.
- ❏ It leads to referrals.
- ❏ It gets you better personal and business service.
- ❏ The people you thank remember you.
- ❏ You stand out from the world of sourpusses everyone meets each day.

The business world spends a fortune on fruit baskets and other corporate gifts. In fact, that's a million-dollar industry in itself. But one personal note is worth much more than a calendar or a pen with your company's name on it.

Watch the papers, television, and magazines for all the ways businesses try to be nice: coupons, giveaways, prizes, sales, promises. Discuss which ones you and your child find effective.

2. Do Something Nice for Someone: How many opportunities did you and your child have to do a good turn today? Write them down. Did you do it? Why? Why not? Philanthropist Milton Gralla, who built a megabusiness starting with $20,000, says, "Nice guys finish first." After publishing trade journals in every industry, he confirms that the folks at the top (although not in the newspapers) constantly do good deeds.

Is a friend out of school? Get them their homework without being asked. Could grandma use a loving phone call? Make it. Is it your mailman's birthday? Send a card.

Note to Parents

Activities 1 and 2 can be done independently of any business your child is in. They are wonderful social habits that naturally enhance business in later years. But if your child does have a hobby, business, sport, or other focus, do the activities in that context. For example, when Arthur tried couponing, he found certain checkout people fast and pleasant, good candidates for thank-yous. He also found coupons that we couldn't use, but that our neighbors with pets could. Good candidates for a good deed.

Did we get any paybacks for our thoughtfulness? In fact, we did. But that's not the point. It's the deed itself that does the trick. Still, when the sign "Cash Register Closed" magically vanishes when Arthur enters the supermarket, it sure cuts down shopping time!

KNOW HOW YOUR BUSINESS IS DOING

3. Keep Records: This book contains examples of lots of different types of records, from invoices to contracts. But, a great experiment is to study something every day for a month with and without record keeping. You and your child will be amazed at the difference in your control and knowledge of the subject when you rely only on memory as compared with documentation.

For example, make a survey of your family's television-watching habits. Who watches what? When do they watch? How do they feel about the program? Try that for one month and share a verbal report with the whole family.

Repeat the survey with a form you create, a time chart, and a viewer-satisfaction questionnaire. At the end of the second month, see how much more you know, how concrete your results are, and how you can use the information to change bad habits, cut down on viewing, increase quality choices, and so on.

4. Write Down Your Business Purpose and Major Profit Center: Especially if you are a hard and dedicated worker, it's easy to forget why you are working. If your child has a business, review with him or her where the most money is made. Connect the effort with the result. For example, if most business comes from one neighborhood, increase efforts in that neighborhood. Go with what works.

If your child is not immediately involved with a business, check out neighborhood businesses. Entrepreneurs love to talk to you. The local bank, restaurant, and dry cleaner will let you know how they see their profit center, where they have made their mistakes, and how they learned to concentrate their efforts in the most effective way.

INNOVATE
5. Think of One New Way People Can Hear of Your Business and Implement It: Balloons, T-shirts, flyers, sky writing—ways to get known are endless. Experiment with your own business. If you don't have a business, keep a list together of all the marketing techniques you and your child noticed throughout the week, from sidewalk sales to radio ads. I bet you come up with at least one new idea in a week's time.

6. Think of One New Way That You Can Make Money and Implement It: It takes creativity to make money. But, an object in motion tends to stay in motion, and a good business tends to expand. If you use a product in your business, can you also manufacture it and sell it to others? Is there a related service you could perform? Why not water the plants while you are baby-sitting?

Look at page 144 of this book, to see how you can help your child become a conglomerate.

BE COST EFFECTIVE

7. Eliminate One Useless or Inefficient Thing You Are Doing: Parents may have a longer list than kids. The list can include business, personal, or social wheel spinning. This exercise often also requires a change in habits. Report to each other on your progress and share the problems of changing your ways.

8. Institute One Time-Saving Device: Do the same as what you did in exercise 7, but concentrate on something that will save you time—learning a new computer skill, using a closer barber, buying in bulk. Time-saving devices sometimes cost money in the beginning but they are worth it.

COMPETE

9. Check the Competition: If your child is in a business with visible competition, help him or her list the things he or she needs to compare: pricing, quality, hours of operation, advertising, and marketing. If there is no business, pick two car dealers, banks, or hair salons in your community and compare them. Which is doing the best? Why?

10. Raise Your Prices! Lower Your Prices! Play Pricing Games. To lower prices, you must buy raw material cheaper, make less of a profit on each item, or lower the quality. Can it be done? Is it worth it? Will it result in higher volume? Are you better off with higher prices for more service, better quality, faster service? Which way is the competition pricing?

Here is my mom's favorite business joke.

Businessperson 1: If you sell balloons at 5 cents each and they cost you 10 cents each, how do you make any money?
Businessperson 2: We make it up on the volume!

Have fun explaining the joke to your kids. I did.

Bibliography

Arthur's Funny Money. Lillian Hoban. New York: Harper & Row Publishers, 1981.

Bernard Baruch. Joanne Landers Henry. New York: Bobbs-Merrill, 1991.

The Best Companies for Women. Baila Zeitz, Ph.D., and Lorraine Dusky. New York: Simon & Schuster, 1988.

Checkbook Management—A Guide to Saving Money. Eric Gelb. Woodmere, N.Y.: Career Advancement Center, Inc., 1994.

Children and Money. Grace W. Weinstein. New York: New American Library, 1985.

Fast Cash for Kids. Bonnie Drew and Noel Drew. Hawthorne, N.J.: Career Press, 1991.

Finding Your First Job. Sue Alexander. New York: E.P. Dutton, 1980.

The First Official Money Making Book for Kids. Fred Shanaman. New York: Bantam Books, 1983.

From Workshop to Toy Store. Richard C. Levy and Ronald O. Weingartner. New York: Simon & Schuster, 1992.

The Great American Gripe Book. Matthew Lesko. Kensington, Md.: Information USA, 1991.

How to Turn Lemons into Money: Money Basics. David Wallace. Englewood Cliffs, N.J.: Prentice-Hall, 1984.

How to Turn Up Into Down Into Up: A Child's Guide to Inflation, Depression, and Economic Recovery. Louise Armstrong. New York: Harcourt Brace Jovanovich, 1976.

How You Can Make a Fortune Selling Information by Mail. Russ von Hoelscher. San Diego, Calif.: Profit Ideas, 1987.

Kid Biz. Bonnie Drew and Noel Drew. Austin, Tex: Eakin Press, 1990.

Kids Biz Game Plan. Cheri Ellison and Debbie Hope. Dana Point, Calif.: ExecuSystems, 1993. A complete system for teaching kids business responsibility in the home without outside jobs; includes contracts, parenting guide, and more. Call 1-800-735-3378.

Moneyskills. Bonnie Drew. Hawthorne, N.J.: Career Press, 1992.

More Free Stuff for Kids. Elizabeth H. Weiss. Deephaven, Minn.: Meadowbrook Press, 1993.

The New Money Workbook for Women. Carole Phillips. Amherst, N.H.: Brick House Publishing, 1988.

New Workbook for Women. Andover, MA, 1982, 1988.

On the Air. Al Parinello. Hawthorne, N.J.: Career Press, 1990.

101 Home Office Success Secrets. Lisa Kanarek. Hawthorne, N.J.: Career Press, 1993.

Publicity Outlets. New Milford, Conn.: Harold Hansen Publishers, 1995

The Rights of Employees. Wayne N. Outten with Noah A. Kinigstein. New York: Bantam Books, 1984.

2 Minute Motivation. Robert W. Wendover. Naperville, Ill.: Sourcebooks, 1995.

Use Your Own Corporation to Get Rich. Judith H. McQuown. New York: Simon & Schuster, 1991.

Your Rights as a Consumer. Marc. R. Lieberman. Hawthorne, N.J.: Career Press, 1994.

Your Wealth-Building Years: Financial Planning for 18-to38-Year-Olds-Third edition. Adriane G. Berg. New York: Newmarket Press, 1995.

About the Authors

ARTHUR BERG BOCHNER at thirteen years old co-authored *The Totally Awesome Business Book* with his mother. Two years earlier, they wrote *The Totally Awesome Money Book for Kids (and Their Parents)*. Arthur was well-received in the press, both television and print, and was featured on "Good Morning America," "Oprah," and "The Tonight Show." Arthur still finds time to invest, research new businesses, collect stamps, and play baseball and chess. He lives in New Jersey.

ADRIANE G. BERG is an attorney, financial planner, licensed stockbroker, and the author of ten books, including, *Your Wealth-Building Years: Financial Planning for 18- to 38-Year-Olds*, known as "one of the best money-management books available" (*New Woman*) and "The best of its kind. First rate." (*Publishers Weekly*) Adriane has written *Financial Planning for Couples: How to Work Together to Build Security and Success* featured as "a no-nonsense guide to help couples start making money decisions that work for them." (*Philadelphia Inquirer*) A host of her own talk show on WABC radio, New York, Adriane is a much sought after speaker and seminar leader.

Index

More Newmarket Press Books for Kids (and Their Parents)

ADRIANE BERG AND ARTHUR BERG BOCHNER
ON MONEY MANAGEMENT

THE TOTALLY AWESOME MONEY BOOK FOR KIDS (AND THEIR PARENTS)

For young readers from ten to seventeen, this fun, fact-filled guide uses quizzes, games, riddles, forms, charts, stories, and drawings, to cover the basics of saving, investing, borrowing, working, and taxes.
"Perfect for kids who want to know what they can do with their money."—*Newsday*

FINANCIAL PLANNING FOR COUPLES
How to Work Together to Build Security and Success—Updated Edition

Berg shows how to make money as a team, covering recordkeeping, budgeting, investment decisions, and much more.

YOUR WEALTH BUILDING YEARS
Financial Planning for 18- to 38-Year-Olds—Third Edition

This invaluable handbook for young adults explains real estate, job benefits, financial instruments, and budgeting in addition to shared housing and socially responsible investing.
"An excellent primer and reference tool...entertaining and informative."—*Nashville Banner*

LYNDA MADARAS ON GROWING UP

THE "WHAT'S HAPPENING TO MY BODY?" BOOK FOR BOYS:
A Growing-Up Guide for Parents and Sons

THE "WHAT'S HAPPENING TO MY BODY?" BOOK FOR GIRLS:
A Growing-Up Guide for Parents and Daughters

MY BODY MY SELF:
The "What's Happening to My Body?" Workbook for Boys

MY BODY MY SELF:
The "What's Happening to My Body?" Workbook for Girls

MY FEELINGS, MY SELF:
Lynda Madaras Growing-Up Guide for Girls